# THE
# YAMPA VALLEY
# SIN CIRCUIT

## Historic Red-Light Districts of Routt and Moffat Counties

## LAUREL WATSON

Charleston · London

THE
History
PRESS

Published by The History Press
Charleston, SC 29403
www.historypress.net

Copyright © 2014 by Laurel L. Watson
All rights reserved

First published 2014

Manufactured in the United States

ISBN 978.1.62619.167.9

Library of Congress CIP data applied for.

# CONTENTS

# Contents

# ACKNOWLEDGEMENTS

I am indebted to a number of people and entities for their help, information and inspiration in compiling this book. For starters, I have to acknowledge the late Mel Hitchens, who put me on the path of this subject a number of years ago, when I was a graduate student working as a bartender in Steamboat Springs. I had no idea what my focus would be for my final project but wanted to research some aspect of local history that had not been extensively looked at. One day, Mel, who must have been in his eighties at the time, was sitting at the bar drinking coffee with a number of local regulars when the subject of the Fifth Street Bridge came up. Being from New Jersey and having relatives from Brooklyn, New York, I thought it was rather peculiar to find a bridge named the Brooklyn Bridge way out here in a small town in Colorado; there had to be a story. Mel, who lived in the little neighborhood called Brooklyn, located across the bridge, started telling me stories about its sordid past, and I was hooked. A mystery and history all wrapped up in one—just the sort of thing that captured my attention. This started my journey of delving into local history that continues today.

I must give credit where credit is due, especially to those historians and authors who came before me and were crucial in preserving the area's history, to whom I cannot express enough gratitude. To them I am especially indebted. Sadly, some passed away many years before I ever had a chance to meet them other than on the pages they have written, while others I had the great fortune to encounter in person. To name just a few of these local historian icons whose writing far exceeds my own, there is Jean Wren; Jan

# Acknowledgements

Leslie; John Leckenby; John Rolf Burroughs; M.S. Merrill; Mike Yurich; the authors, compilers and contributors of *The History of Hayden & West Routt County 1876–1989*, including Pat Holderness and Judy and Jerry Green; and the authors of *The Historical Guide to Routt County*, Jim Stanko, Sureva Towler and Judy Seligson. These are the "pioneers" of preserving the local area history, and I am forever in their debt. I would like to also thank the Frentress (Durbin) family, who shared family stories, photos and records with me, giving me insight into a dead end that I ran across in research.

The following stories could not have been compiled without the wonderful help of the local area museums and personnel whose invaluable insight and help with photos I could not have done without. Thank you to Dan Davidson, Jan Gerber and Mary Pat Dunn of the Museum of Northwest Colorado; the Hayden Heritage Center in Hayden; Nita Naugle and Mike Yurich from Tracks & Trails Museum in Oak Creek; Rita Herald from the Yampa Historical Society; and Candice Bannister and Katie Adams from the Tread of Pioneers Museum in Steamboat Springs.

I would like to give a special acknowledgement to local historians Paul and Ellen Bonnifield, who provided information and encouragement and helped me gain a better understanding of this period of time while giving me information I may never have found.

I also must acknowledge History Colorado and its wonderful website for Colorado historic newspapers, which is a fantastic resource for a wealth of information. Also, I would like to thank the Colorado Archives archivist who dug through prison records and multiples of common names; even in this digital age, it can be a cumbersome job. I would like to thank my editor, Becky LeJeune, who has patiently put up with me through this, my first project. And speaking of patience, I would also like to thank my husband and children, who have supported me throughout this project and continually put up with my fascination with the past, and my mother-in-law, Patti Watson, who shares my love of history and genealogy.

This book is dedicated to those individuals throughout the past whose history and lives have been left unrecorded.

# INTRODUCTION

This book is by no means a comprehensive study on the saloons and saloon people of Northwest Colorado. There were so many saloons, businesses and individuals who owned, worked and lived in these areas and came and went during the period in which this book covers that it proved too daunting a task to discover and research each and every person. Instead, this is a sampling of some of the more notable characters and stories of the period, an insert to the local historical record. I have included very brief histories to try to give some background information to help in the understanding of the subject matter, as you cannot look at any aspect of history without looking at the surrounding circumstances.

The history of many red-light districts of western towns has typically been omitted from original references due to the fact that they were considered of an objectionable nature by the dominant Victorian cultural social mores and strict sexual conventions of the later nineteenth and early twentieth centuries. This stigmatization created a problem in the lack of earlier attention to documentation of areas and businesses that were considered red-light or saloon districts, which generally contained business from saloons, gambling halls, billiard rooms and boardinghouses of illicit reputation to residential areas of the working class, immigrants and people of color. In some towns, only residual references have been left for the historical record. Due to the lack of any comprehensive records, this is a limited document giving an overview of the development and brief biographies of some of the individuals who lived and worked in these places and any interesting stories that I came across during my research. These were people who came from somewhat diverse backgrounds, yet they were similar. The individuals who lived and worked in these districts and businesses were the remnants of a period of social wildness that transcended the moral implications of the period. They were an embodiment of the rampant American capitalistic entrepreneurialism that constituted the period of expansionism at the end of the Gilded Age just as Progressive-era reforms were emerging across America. Their stories are like many other Americans' during any time period; while some found success and fortune, others found failure and dismal disappointment. Nevertheless, their story is part of the epoch called the American West.

*What is the chief end of man? To get rich. In what way? Dishonestly if we can; honestly if we must.*
—Mark Twain, 1871

During the period that this book covers, America was going through one of its greatest economic growth spurts. Industry was booming, and it was the age of the tycoons, or robber barons, such as Rockefeller, Carnegie and Morgan, businessmen whose wealth exceeded any before them. This was also the period in which America would see the largest waves of immigrants come to its shores in search of the American dream of prosperity, only to find poverty and overcrowded living conditions in the tenements of the cities in which they landed.

The Homestead Act of 1862, enacted during the Civil War, would come to the forefront as a catalyst for western expansion. The United States had acquired large portions of western lands during the early 1800s. First there was the Louisiana Purchase in 1805, which almost doubled the size of the United States. Then it acquired even more territory from Mexico after the Mexican-American War ended in 1848 with the Treaty of Guadalupe Hidalgo. This gave the United States everything north of the Rio Grande formerly owned by Mexico, including the modern areas of California, New Mexico, Utah and parts of Colorado and Wyoming. Political and economic issues hampered the development of these newly acquired territories, as did the lack of clear homestead legislation setting up a means for citizens to acquire lands. Although some made the journey westward and filed hazy preemption claims for land, the majority stayed in the East, where the country had just begun to industrialize and eastern cities provided more promising economic opportunities than a land that was full of dangers and impediments. The difficulties between the states leading up to the Civil War hampered development of land legislation. Neither the Northern nor

Southern states wanted new territories settled, as any new states would disrupt the delicate balance of free and slave states. The outbreak of the Civil War finally allowed for the passage of the Homestead Act in 1862. This legislation basically enabled any adult who could pay a small filing fee, live on the land for five years and make basic improvements to the home site to file for 160 acres in the newly opened western lands.

Conditions after the Civil War were just right for western expansion to take off, as there was a number of people looking for land and new opportunities. The largest influx of immigrants would come to the United States during this period of time. There were also multitudes of landless and displaced people in the wake of the war, such as freed ex-slaves. To top it off, there were those looking to make money by speculation, mining or other means. The frontiers of the West, with their abundant land and undeveloped wealth, offered a new horizon of opportunity for anyone daring enough to take a chance and go west.

Towns popped up across the American West as the lands were wrested from the Native American people, and progress steamed its way across the continent in the form of the transcontinental railroad. Most towns developed due to some aspect of their locations that promised economic prosperity, whether it was a transportation hub, a mine strike, an agricultural center or some form of speculative enterprise. These early western towns developed somewhat differently than their eastern counterparts, as they were dominantly male and openly lenient toward the moral attributes of their inhabitants. Thus, the saloon became the lifeblood of the western town, as it was the place of solace and entertainment to many lonely miners, railroad builders and cowboys. Gradually, western society became more domesticated as more women and families moved westward and towns became more connected with the East with the construction of the railroad. Moral standards were subsequently established that coincided with the dominant Victorian social mores of the developed East, which delegated immoral behavior and those who participated in professions considered immoral to the edge of society.

For a time, many western towns adopted the quiet acceptance of controlling immoral behaviors such as drinking, gambling and prostitution by separating those types of businesses from good society, creating separate areas of town generally known as saloon districts or red-light districts. These ranged from being completely separate areas of a town to certain areas of a business district to individual buildings in a town's business district.

The saloon was considered an established entity of the American West and a moneymaker for not only the proprietors who owned them but also the counties or towns in which they were located. In Colorado, it was up to the counties or the incorporated towns to decide whether to allow alcohol and to set license fees and bonds while adhering to state law. If a town was unincorporated, it was up to the county commissioners to set those fees, collect the monies and spend them as they saw fit. It was in the best interest of a town that had saloons to incorporate in order to add to its town treasuries. Saloons, grocery stores and pharmacies that sold liquor for medicinal purposes each paid high fees and bonds for licenses to sell alcohol. These monies enabled fledgling counties or towns to utilize the large amounts of money generated by these "immoral" businesses to help build necessary infrastructure such as bridges, roads and ditches.

The men who owned saloons generally had varied business interests, investing in multitudes of different enterprises. They were considered businessmen, and although their business was objectionable to some, they still could walk both sides of the road of acceptability in society. Many were even politically active. Women of the red-light districts, or prostitutes, however, were treated as social pariahs, labeled as "known women." No respectable woman or man would publicly have anything to do with these women, who were considered the dredges of society. Respectable women would cross streets to avoid such women, shielding their children's eyes and avoiding any contact lest any of their sinful ways should rub off on them or their children. Many towns did not even like acknowledging the presence of such women. One creative census recorder in an early Colorado mining town was either feeling humorous or very embarrassed when he listed the abundant number of local prostitutes with bogus jobs such as "ceiling inspector," "mattress demonstrator" and "horizontal worker." Prostitutes knew theirs was a shameful, lonely life, and most changed their names so that distant family members would not have to deal with the shame. Many prostitutes who had children opted to send them away to distant boarding schools so that they were not exposed to their mothers' profession and the social stigma it would bring upon them.

Not everyone was happy with the quiet acquiescence of these districts, even for monetary gain for public benefit, as they were seen as the denizens of social ills that plagued society. The independent attitudes and desire for a better life that brought many westward acted as a stimulus for many reform-minded individuals to speak up on the issue not only on a social level but also on a political level. One of the more powerful social reform movements that swept through the American West was the temperance movement, which abhorred the consumption of alcohol because it was seen as a destroyer of families. Towns such as Greeley, Colorado, were even founded on structured temperance ideals that sought to improve society by ridding it of vice such as alcohol, gambling and illicit behavior.

# Part I
# VALLEY OF DREAMS

# Chapter 1

# NORTHWEST COLORADO

The mountainous ranges and wide grass parks and valleys of northwestern Colorado were some of the last western frontier lands opened to white settlement in the late 1860s. Although settled later than many other parts of the American West, the area went through all the same developing stages, starting with early exploration, mining rushes, Indian removal, influx of homesteaders, cattle drives, railroad ambitions and the development of towns.

Some of the first people to arrive and settle in the area straddled along the Little Snake area of the southern Wyoming Territory since only pockets of land were open to white settlement. The western slope part of the Colorado Territory, almost one-third of the territory, was given to the Utes through treaty. The Treaty of 1868 with the Utes opened up a stretch of Northwest Colorado, now Moffat and Routt Counties, to the Utah state line and pushed the Northern Ute Indians southward to Rio Blanco County.

In 1873, Ferdinand V. Hayden, under the sponsorship of the federal government, brought his geological survey team through the Northwest Colorado Territory and up into the Wyoming Territory to map and survey the various elements of the terrain. His team consisted of notable scientists and naturalists of the day and included the famous photographer William H. Jackson. Hayden's extensive volumes of *The U.S. Geological and Geographical Survey of the Territories* noted the region's significant mineral wealth, as well as the flora and fauna. His findings were of special interest to not only the government but also the railroad companies, as well as eastern investors.

Hayden's findings documented a wealth of ores and minerals in Northwest Colorado, particularly coal, and a land good for agricultural pursuits—tall grasses for livestock and water for irrigation—as well as abundant wildlife.

Although natural wealth abounded in Northwest Colorado territory, it was still slow to develop, mostly due to its remote location in the rugged mountains. By 1875, seven years after the area was open to settlement, only twenty-three families lived in the newly opened lands scattered across Northwest Colorado to Utah.[1]

The proximity of the Ute White River Reservation was another deterrent to the settlement of the area. The situation at the reservation had been slowly deteriorating during the 1870s. The Utes were continually plagued by the failure of the U.S. government to provide necessary rations promised to them, which led to many of the Utes going off the reservation to hunt to provide food for their families. This led to difficulties with homesteaders who complained to the authorities. Things seemed to improve for a period after the appointment of the idealistic Nathan Meeker as the reservation agent in 1878, but it was short-lived. Meeker's inexperience and overbearing idealism led to problems that escalated to violence. The resistance of many of the younger tribesmen to convert to a sedentary agricultural lifestyle was a problem that caused tension between them and Agent Meeker. Meeker's insistence on plowing a field used by the Utes to pasture their prized ponies through the long winter caused a confrontation between him and a tribesman by the name of Johnson. Meeker was publicly insulted when Johnson physically pushed him during an argument. Bitter that the Utes would not adhere to his plans, he told one of the native girls who worked at the agency that the Utes did not own their land and that the government could take it if they did not use it as he directed. This only created resentment and fear, as well as uncertainty throughout the agency.

In a poorly calculated move to get the Utes to adhere to his plans, Meeker sent for troops to intercede. Memories of the Sand Creek Massacre of 1864, in which troops attacked and mercilessly slaughtered the Black Kettle group of Cheyennes while they were supposedly under the protection of peace talks, were still fresh in the minds of the Utes. The sight of advancing troops, a direct violation of Article 2 of the 1868 treaty, only panicked the already fearful Utes. Violence finally erupted on September 29, 1878, as troops headed toward the agency. The troops were not far from the agency when an unknown shot was fired, sparking the four-day siege of Milk Creek that left Major Thornburgh, who headed the troops, twelve soldiers and around forty-three Utes dead. Word of the battle would quickly pass on to the

The mining town of Hahn's Peak. Note the three saloons. *Museum of Northwest Colorado.*

Hahn's Peak Fourth of July celebration, circa 1907. *Hayden Heritage Center.*

agency, where violence would break out, leaving Nathan Meeker killed along with the ten civilian men who worked at the agency. Meeker's wife, Arvilla; his daughter Josephine; and the wife of one of the workers, Flora Price, and her two small children became captives of the Utes for over twenty-three days until their release was negotiated by Chief Ouray of the Southern Ute band. News of the ensuing violence at the agency led many of the area homesteaders to flee, some never to return. In the aftermath, the Utes lost much of their coveted Colorado lands, and the tribes from the White River Reservation were removed to the Unitah Reservation in Utah, allowing more lands to be opened for homesteading and mineral development.

During the 1880s, after the removal of the Utes, a number of homesteaders arrived in the area, and eventually towns developed. Deposits of gold and silver sparked the early development of the mining town of Hahn's Peak,

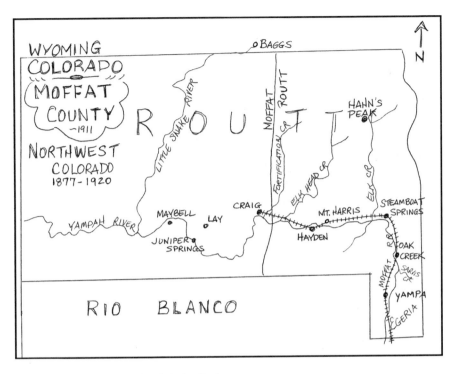

Map of Northwest Colorado. *Author's collection.*

which was the seat of Routt County from 1878 to 1912. Hahn's Peak was a lively little town with a few saloons that eventually dwindled as the mines panned out by the 1890s. Meanwhile, other towns developed, such as Yampa, Steamboat Springs, Hayden and Craig.

The catalyst for the region's growth came after March 1902, when newspapers across the state were reporting that Denver banking magnate and entrepreneur David H. Moffat had revealed his elaborate plan to run railroad track from Denver to Salt Lake City through Northwest Colorado. According to an Associated Press telegram, Moffat's new road would connect in Salt Lake City with Senator W.A. Clark's San Pedro, Los Angeles & Salt Lake City Railway.[2] This would not only create a direct line from Denver to Salt Lake City but would also connect Denver directly to the West Coast, allowing Moffat to tap the wealth of Routt County coal, cattle and grain. Moffat proceeded to construct his line, and by June 1902, the first ten miles heading toward the mountains from Arvada to Coal Creek were almost done. Moffat surveyor and engineer teams set out to survey the best path to Routt County. By the following year, over three thousand

Track layers, circa 1913. *Hayden Heritage Center.*

Mount Harris, circa 1915. *Hayden Heritage Center.*

men were employed in laying track through the mountains. Moffat was well on his way to his goal of laying track through Routt County. According to Moffat himself, "Northwestern Colorado is a treasure house upon the doors of which nature has placed locks and bars. The Moffat road will supply the key by which these treasures will be made available."[3]

Other towns developed and thrived with the common thread of the influence of the railroad, which sparked speculative economic booms and rapid development in the towns that were to be along its path. Towns such as Oak Creek and Phippsburg were built to accommodate the influx of miners, railroad workers and settlers who poured into the area. Later, there were the company-owned mining towns of Mount Harris, McGregor and Bear River, founded by large fuel companies that built their own towns to house their workers who toiled in the large mines gleaning the rich beds of coal once deemed Routt County gold. These company towns became possible after the railroad laid its tracks.

In 1911, Moffat County was carved out of the westernmost portion of Routt County, with the town of Craig as its county seat. Regardless of this split, the newly formed county was still closely associated with Routt County. If not politically, it was still linked geographically, being located in the same Yampa Valley and on the same line of the Moffat Railroad.

Saloons, like trading posts, were some of the first establishments erected at stopping points for travelers and settlers. One of the first saloons was constructed by John Jarvie, a Scotsman who settled in the Browns Park area and established a trading post and ferry service. Most of the towns that emerged in Northwest Colorado had their own version of a saloon district. Some were simply saloons with gambling, while others ran prostitutes as well. Steamboat Springs' red-light district was separate from town, while others, like Oak Creek, were incorporated into their town's business center and situated on their main streets. Many of the individuals whose survival relied on these saloons and brothels moved about these towns, popping up from town to town depending on the prospects of wealth or trouble with town officials. The following is the result of weaving together oral histories, memoirs, newspaper stories and records from the period to try to piece together a look at these colorful establishments and characters of Northwest Colorado.

# Part II
# A Town Divided

# Chapter 2
# STEAMBOAT SPRINGS

S teamboat Springs is a resort town known for its beautiful scenery, numerous mineral springs, Olympic skiing tradition, outdoor recreation and western town charm and hospitality, yet few realize that it once was a dry community complete with its own notorious red-light district. The small, quiet neighborhood called Brooklyn, which is tucked behind the ice rink and rodeo grounds across the Yampa River to the southeast, was once a notorious hamlet of bawdy and illicit behavior, complete with rowdy saloons, loose women and even outlaws.

The earliest legends of the area state that French trappers had been visiting the Yampa Valley area, where the present-day site of Steamboat Springs sits, since the early 1860s and had commonly referred to the small valley of numerous mineral springs as Steamboat Springs. They called it Steamboat Springs because one of the mineral springs near the Yampa River, sometimes also referred to as the Bear River, made a chugging noise reminiscent of the sounds that a river steamboat made.[4] The area remained relatively untouched by white civilization while other parts of the West were being developed because it was originally considered Ute Indian lands by treaty. By 1875, a permanent settlement was created near present-day Steamboat Springs when James Crawford brought his young family from Nebraska to stake a homestead.[5] Other homesteaders followed Crawford's lead, such as the Bennetts and the Woolerys.[6] The Woolerys eventually set up a roadhouse near the Yampa River in what is now the downtown area of Steamboat Springs. These early settlers lived in a peaceful, sometimes uncomfortable coexistence with the neighboring Utes at the White River Reservation. The proximity of the reservation and the remoteness of the town, however, deterred growth of the town at first.

After the Ute removal in the early 1880s, the Woolery roadhouse prospered due to the influx of numerous miners to the Hahn's Peak gold mine camp to the north, as well as the multitudes of homesteaders who were flocking to the newly open rangelands to the west. As other families settled in the Steamboat Valley, it was only a matter of time before a town would be erected to meet their needs.

James Crawford saw that the valley area of Steamboat Springs was a perfect stopping spot for travelers who were coming and going to the various locales in the Upper Yampa River area, and he set out to get financial backing to form a town. In 1885, Crawford and businessmen J.P. Maxwell, Andrew Mackay and several others from Boulder formed the Steamboat Town Site Company and planned out streets, alleyways and town lots.[7] Within three short years, the town grew from five buildings to more than forty.[8] Although the gold placer mines in Hahn's Peak were played out by the 1890s, the steady flow of new immigrants did not slow down. Agriculture was the new boom, and the Yampa and Elk Valleys were found to have rich soil and plenty of water for irrigation purposes. With the Homestead Act making land affordable to anyone daring enough to take up a homestead, people began to pour into the region.

Rumors grew that the banking and railroad magnate David Moffat was planning to build a railroad through the Yampa Valley to Salt Lake City, which caused even more people to flock to the area and especially to the town of Steamboat. Steamboat was already a hub for agriculture and cattle even before it became a railway thoroughfare since it was already the natural stopping point for the stagecoach, as well as cattle drivers and farmers who were on their way to and from Northwest Colorado via the nearest railroad stations such as the Denver Rio Grande & Western Line in Wolcott, Colorado, or the Union Pacific Line in Rawlins, Wyoming. The building of Moffat's Denver Northwestern & Pacific Railway line connecting Denver to Salt Lake via Northwest Colorado with a main station at Steamboat Springs would mean even greater prosperity and opportunities for the region since this would connect it with two major cities as markets for the area's goods, as well as make it more accessible for travelers. The numerous mineral springs, along with the arid western mountain climate, meant that Steamboat was also a haven for health seekers and tourists, and the addition of a passenger train would enable tourism to become a cornerstone in the town's economic structure. The only problem was that the Denver Northwestern & Pacific Line had two options for its construction westward. One of these routes was through Twenty Mile Park to Hayden, leaving Steamboat as a branch line, and the other was through Oak Creek to Steamboat, with Steamboat as a major terminal.[9] The people of Steamboat Springs were determined to have the railroad built directly through town, and as an inducement, they donated over $40,000 in land and cash to persuade the railroad's decision in their favor.[10] With the promising future of the railroad construction through town, a growing boom in agriculture and discoveries of coal shale deposits and oil in the area, Steamboat Springs was a beacon of opportunity for any entrepreneurial individual.

In 1900, as the settlement began to grow larger, the founders of Steamboat Springs incorporated the northern side of the Yampa River as the town of Steamboat Springs and set up rules and regulations. The first of these were outlined in the *Pilot* newspaper in an article that was published on November 21, 1900. Simply headlined as "Ordinance," the article stated the prohibition of alcohol sales within town limits and set fees for liquor establishments within their proximity to town limits.[11] These alcohol prohibitions were also embedded into each property deed. Crawford and other town founders were temperance minded or what the late John R. Burroughs, who was a writer of local history, would call "straight laced folks" who developed the town's charter based on the ideals of Horace Greeley, which included temperance clauses that prohibited the sale, purchase or consumption of any intoxicants within the city limits.[12] Every deed issued for real estate in Steamboat contained a no-liquor restriction that was passed along to each purchaser until it was rescinded by a ruling by the Colorado Supreme Court in 1940.[13] Although the founders of Steamboat were very temperance-minded individuals, they recognized that not all the residents and visitors of northwestern Colorado were similar. They realized that establishing a strict temperance town might detract non-temperance-minded visitors and wealthy investors and that the monies from these establishments could help build the town infrastructure. In order to establish a thriving metropolis that catered to a variety of individuals including railroad workers, cowboys and tourists, they amended their high standards to allow a resort district, or red-light district, to be built near the town yet separated by the river commonly referred to as Brooklyn.

The city of Steamboat Springs, Colorado, was incorporated in 1900 on temperance ideals. Any saloons previously located within the main town were required to either adhere to the standards for a temperance saloon or

The hot springs looking west, circa 1900s. *Tread of Pioneers Museum.*

close their doors and move outside the incorporated city area. Most picked up and moved their businesses just across the river to the neighborhood that would come to be known as Brooklyn.

In Steamboat Springs, little has remained of this notorious Brooklyn red-light district or the people who worked and lived there. Although some of the characters in Brooklyn were colorful enough to fit the Hollywood depictions, most of the individuals who lived and worked there were just ordinary people trying to make their fortunes or survive the best way they could. The remnants of the Brooklyn red-light district are all but gone; the buildings have long since been either demolished or refurbished, leaving little evidence that a commercial district even existed. The only monuments left to commemorate this once notorious hamlet are the nickname of the Fifth Street Bridge as the Brooklyn Bridge and the subdivision sign noting "Entering Historic Brooklyn." Not only did the neighborhood slip into obscurity, but so did the people who were once notoriously well known and lived and worked there.

# Chapter 3

# STEAMBOAT SPRINGS
# RED-LIGHT DISTRICT

## BROOKLYN

S ince no alcohol was allowed in downtown Steamboat Springs, a number of drinking establishments were erected outside town limits. Many of these were on the south side of the Yampa River. This was just outside the incorporated town of Steamboat Springs, which meant it was outside the deeded liquor-restricted area. Originally, this section of land, directly across the river from the town of Steamboat, was part of one of the Woolery brothers' homesteads. In 1899, when rumors began to circulate that the railroad would lay tracks to Salt Lake City through northwestern Colorado with Steamboat Springs as a possible major terminal, Joseph Woolery saw the possibilities of a financial boom and had part of his homestead platted into small town lots.

This area was first called the Woolery addition to Steamboat in deed records and land transfers. In 1903, lots in the Woolery addition were being advertised by the Niesz Wheeler Realty Company at a going rate of twenty-five dollars each.[14] In 1907, it seems that there was a rush to try to incorporate the neighborhood, with the possibility of creating a "new town" out of Steamboat before the train arrived; however, nothing came of it. Thirteen more lots were platted near the river, each measuring 25 by 125 feet.[15] Saloons were the dominant businesses since the area was outside the deed restrictions, and the monies from the subsequent liquor licenses would be used in "beautifying the park on both sides of the river" in preparation

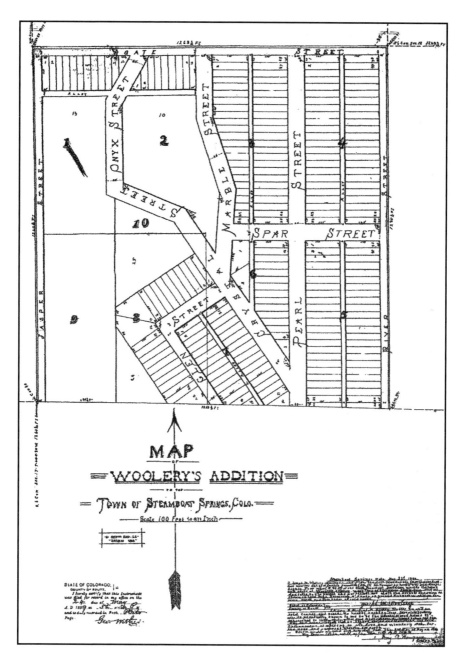

Woolery's addition to Steamboat Springs (Brooklyn) plat map, circa 1908. *Courtesy Routt County Records.*

*Left*: Brooklyn Bridge sign. *Author's collection.*

*Below*: Brooklyn Bridge. *Author's collection.*

for the arrival of the railroad.[16] There were other businesses besides the saloons, including boardinghouses, a bottling company, an icehouse, cafés and a blacksmith shop, as well as a number of family homes. However, this neighborhood became known locally and regionally as a recreation spot of vice commonly referred to as a red-light district.

According to the late John R. Burroughs, legend had it that the little red-light district of saloons and brothels that lay across the Second Street bridge was named Brooklyn by an alcoholic and consumptive artist originally from New York City who "possessed a sense of humor and a flair for liquor, women, and oil paints in that order."[17] Brooklyn, as it was thus called, was originally connected to town by a small wooden bridge that crossed the Yampa River connecting it to Second Street, which is approximately near the current bike path bridge that crosses the river behind the Rabbit Ears Motel. This route was also used as the stagecoach road that ran to Oak Creek, Yampa and Wolcott. When the new bridge on Fifth Street was built, it was aptly christened the Brooklyn Bridge.

Although the proprietors of the saloon establishments had to petition for liquor licenses, they found that the town leaders were quite willing to grant them. It seemed the good citizens of Steamboat were initially content that the area existed because it served to appease the rowdy cowboys who came into town off the range on paydays looking for a drink and some unrestrained fun. Incidents of violence on the streets of town by drunken cowboys especially helped the mindset of citizens of Steamboat to agree to the development of a saloon district across the river. One of the most prominent incidents occurred on July 19, 1894, when a drunken cowboy by the name of Joseph Pace, who had been drinking all day in a local saloon that was located on the present-day site of the Old Courthouse, recklessly started shooting his gun in the air. He accidentally shot and killed a young boy by the name of Samuel McFadden who happened to be across the street.[18] Moving the saloons to the other side of the river relegated the cowboys and their offensive, and often violent, behavior across the river and off the streets of the town proper.

Brooklyn's actual beginnings as a red-light district are somewhat foggy since there were no regulations on saloons prior to the town's incorporation and subsequent development of ordinances in the early 1900s, so there were saloons both in and around town. According to an interview conducted in 1982 by Nancy Hoar for *The Three Wire Winter* magazine with lifetime resident Dorothy Wither, 1885 appears to be the year that the first official saloon was built, "when her father brought the first load of liquor over the pass."[19] However, according to another interviewee, local Bob Swinehart, the first saloon was constructed in 1898.[20] Regardless, over the next fifteen years, a number of saloons were built.

W.E. Harris had one of the early saloons before his wife divorced him and he sold out. Some of the other saloons that dotted the Brooklyn neighborhood included the Bottle Works, which was opened by a Mr. Olsen. Then there was also the Waunita Bar and the Oasis, a few of the saloons started by Gus Durbin and the highly respected Capital Saloon owned by Anton Kline. Another proprietor of saloons was Shorty Anderson, who built two saloons, the Mint Saloon and the Antlers Saloon.

In addition to saloons, billiard halls, cafés, hotels and rooming houses were also constructed to meet the demands of an ever-growing town. The brothels were nicely referred to as "rooming houses," "hotels" or "boardinghouses for girls" by the citizens of Steamboat, as well as their own inhabitants in census records. According to the *Routt County Sentinel*, there was a total of four "sporting houses" in Brooklyn in 1909.[21] Rarely were women ever called prostitutes or any of the other colorful euphemism such as "demimonde" or "soiled dove" in the local newspapers; instead, they were referred to as "known women of Brooklyn" or "inmates of Brooklyn." Like at other railroad stops, small houses dotted the neighborhood that ran near the tracks, in which various loose women plied their trade. Other forms of entertainment, such as gambling, billiards and live music, could be found at any of the various saloons in Brooklyn.

With the incorporation of the town of Steamboat Springs, only temperance saloons could be established on the town side of the Yampa River. Saloons that carried whiskey and other vinous liquors had to relegate themselves to across the river. In 1900, the town board established an ordinance that outlined licensing fees for both types of saloons. Temperance saloons had to pay $75 per year, while saloons doing business across the river had to pay $500 per year.[22] Drugstores also had to pay a liquor fee since alcohol could be purchased legally for medicinal purposes within town limits at these establishments. The fee for drugstores was set at $125 per year. Alcohol ordinances were on the town board docket quite regularly throughout the years. In June 1901, a new ordinance regulating alcohol sales was passed, reading as follows:

> *To sell any liquors, intoxicating or not, within town limits or one mile beyond the same $500 per year. Druggists may be granted licenses to sell in quantities of less than five gallons, for medicinal, mechanical, and chemical purposes only on payment of $50 per year. Druggists must keep a record of each sale, giving name of purchaser, use for which liquor is intended, etc.*

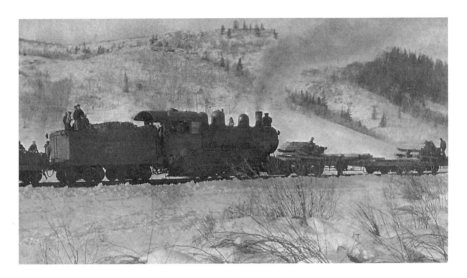

The first train to Steamboat, circa 1908. Howelson Hill is in the background, and Brooklyn was to the left. *Hayden Heritage Center.*

Brooklyn neighborhood sign. *Author's collection.*

*Billiard halls and temperance saloons must pay $400 per year. A bond of $2000 must be deposited with each application for license.*[23]

Fines for violating the ordinance on licensing were also established during this town meeting, which set the punishment from $25 to $300.[24] Although the fees to set up a saloon seemed hefty at a time when the average salary was about $30 a month, a number of establishments were erected and licensed in Brooklyn.

In 1908, the railroad laid tracks through Steamboat Springs along the Yampa River on the Brooklyn side, allowing for Brooklyn to become even more prosperous. The saloons and bawdyhouses catered to the railroad workers who were living in a makeshift camp of tents set up near the river on the Brooklyn side. Other businesses, such as the limekiln and sawmills, prospered near Brooklyn, where their workers, many of whom were immigrants and male, lived. The neighborhood thrived, quietly for the most part, and many businesses and infamous people came and went throughout its heyday, which ran roughly between 1902 and 1916.

# Chapter 4

# ENTERTAINMENT BROOKLYN STYLE

In a time when there was no television or radio, town events played a major role as entertainment and relaxation, as well as excitement for residents of the area. Town events gave the hardworking settlers time to get together with old friends, as well as make new acquaintances. These events also served as a means, besides the mineral springs, to draw tourists to the town, especially after the construction of the railroad. Despite Brooklyn being considered a denizen of wickedness, a number of town festivities were organized by the "saloon bunch," and most events took place on the Brooklyn side of the Yampa River due to the large open field that served as a stockholding area, as well as rodeo grounds, baseball fields and a site for various festival events.

## RODEO

The organized rodeo of modern days grew out of the impromptu bucking and racing contests that cowboys would hold on the spur of the moment when they came to town off the range. Cowboys worked long and hard on the open range, and when they finally got paid, they headed to town, where their behavior was often riotous. They played as hard as they worked, often showing off their range skills, especially when it came to breaking and racing horses. On a moment's notice, they would race one another up and down town streets or hold bucking contests.

Bucking contests were especially dangerous on town streets, as the rider had little to no control over the violently bucking horse. Cowboys used a technique called snubbing, where they would tie an unbroken horse's front legs between its rear legs, making the horse go to a kneeling position, which would allow a rider to mount the horse on the ground. They would then release the ropes on the horse, at which time it would jump up with the rider on its back and proceed to buck violently. There was no "ten-second rule" back then; riders stayed on the horse until they were thrown or the horse stopped bucking.

These antics proved to be a nuisance in the growing town. The Steamboat Springs Board of Trustees finally got fed up with the cowboys' antics and in August 1903 passed an ordinance, as printed in the *Routt County Sentinel*, which provided:

> *Sec 1. That no person shall ride or drive any horse or horses, ass or asses, or other animal or animals, within the limits of the town of Steamboat Springs at a speed greater than at the rate of ten miles per hour.*
>
> *Sec. 2 (a). No person or persons shall break or attempt to break, ride or attempt to ride any wild, vicious, pitching, or bucking horse, ass, bronco, or other animal or animals within the streets of said town...*

George Bird on Wherlwind in Steamboat Springs. Notice the wooley chaps, a favorite of Northwest Colorado cowboys circa the late 1910s. *Hayden Heritage Center.*

*Sec 3. The mayor is hereby authorized upon any public occasions to permit fast riding and driving, the breaking and riding of wild and pitching horses, asses, or broncos in that part of town of Steamboat Springs south of the Bear River (now known as the Yampa River) and west of Pearl Street.*[25]

This ordinance relegated the cowboys' rambunctious horsing around to the Brooklyn side of the river. Here, a number of local cowboys tried their luck on the bucking broncos; however, the most famous to come out of the Steamboat rodeo scene was not a cowboy but rather a horse by the name of Pin Ears. Pin Ears was a famous bucking horse owned by a local rancher named Lou Long. Pin Ears was known as the "Routt County Terror" and was so popular for bucking contests that he was one of the bucking broncos in the Denver Exhibition in 1905.[26]

# BASEBALL

Baseball was quickly becoming a national phenomenon as well as a favorite local pastime. Town rivalry had already existed since the days leading up to the construction of the railroad and the vying for railroad terminals. Baseball was no different. Each town developed its own team of nine players that competed with other towns in the region. Some towns, like Glenwood Springs, supported their town teams; however, most teams were like Steamboat's and were supported by the members themselves and from game ticket revenues.

The baseball fields were located on the Brooklyn side of the river near the present-day rodeo grounds and softball fields. This was a convenient spot because it had a fairly level, open field close to town and was close to cold beer in the Brooklyn saloons after the game.

In 1914, the Bear River Colorado Baseball League was formed by the towns of Steamboat Springs, Hayden, Yampa, Craig and Phippsburg.[27] These leagues had both adult teams as well as junior teams. Games were played quite regularly and were included in any festival or town celebration as a major event. Competition ran deep, and not only among rival towns. The two rival newspapers, the *Routt County Sentinel* and the *Pilot*, also got into the action with teams of their own competing against each other. In 1904, the two editors—Weiskopf of the *Routt County Sentinel* and Leckenby of the *Pilot*—made a strange bet not only that the loser had to shave off his

A baseball game in Steamboat, circa 1900s. *Tread of Pioneers Museum.*

moustache and let the Ladies' Aid societies of the ME and Congregational church publish the paper for a week but also that he could not mention the word "booze" for three months in his newspaper.[28] Had the two teams tied, neither one could have mentioned "booze" for three months, which, according to the *Elbert County Banner*, would have "probably driven the saloon keepers of that town into bankruptcy."[29] For the record, the *Routt County Sentinel* won the game in the last inning with a score of 13–10.[30]

# FESTIVALS

Festivals such as the Pioneer Days, Fourth of July celebration events, Carnival, Game Days and the Strawberry Festival also occurred on the Brooklyn side of the river. These acted as another means of drawing tourists to Steamboat Springs, especially after the construction of the railroad.

Pioneer Days was a unique event that lasted two days and included rodeo events, horse races, foot races, fireworks, picnics and a parade and concluded with a grand ball. This not only served as a means of gathering old-timers for remembrance of bygone days but also acted as a tourist attraction, drawing thousands of people. Pioneer Days grew out of the development of the community organization called the Routt County Pioneer Association. In 1903, James Crawford organized a meeting of

Pioneer Day Rodeo at the rodeo grounds in Steamboat Springs on the Brooklyn side of the river. *Hayden Heritage Center.*

early settlers to form an association to both preserve a historical record as well as serve as a way for early settlers to see their old friends again, as stated in the preamble of the Pioneer Association constitution: "The object of this association shall be the promotion of social and friendly relations among the pioneers of Routt County, Colorado. And to bring out more extensively and minutely its early history."[31]

Other events occurred over the years, such as Game Days, in which hunters killed various local game, which was then cooked at an elaborate feast, or the Strawberry Festival, which included all-you-could-eat local strawberries and fresh cream. Of course, the annual Fourth of July festival included fireworks. Regardless of the type of festival the town hosted, they each generally included baseball games, dances and various competitions, including rodeo events.

The Brooklyn side of the river also served as a convenient camping spot for some of the numerous people who came to town for the festivities.

# BOXING MATCHES

The "manly art of self-defense," or prizefighting, has been around since the time of the Greeks; however, it saw a resurgence in popularity in the 1800s and was quickly becoming a popular sport to gamble on. Across the United States, saloons and athletic clubs, many of which were formed partly as a means to legitimize such events, became the natural venue for these matches. At the turn of the century, boxing rules were few; participants wore the equivalent of well-padded mittens and fought until an opponent ceded or was knocked out. Most saloon matches followed loose adaptions of the Queensbury rules, and matches were more a test of endurance, sometimes going fifteen or more rounds, rather than skill.[32] Although gambling was officially illegal, private bets were placed, and matches were able to be publicized as exhibition fights purely for entertainment purposes. A number of well-publicized matches occurred in Brooklyn and other towns in Northwest Colorado, many being sparked by the competitiveness of different towns with one another, so each town had its own favorites.

## Chapter 5

# BROOKLYN SALOONKEEPERS

The saloon was a mainstay of the western American town. In the early days of expansion, the saloon was the social hub for the many men who went westward to make their fortunes. Some of these first saloons were nothing more than makeshift tents set up in the mining camps that sprang up almost overnight where a gold or silver strike was found, while others were more permanent structures such as trading posts along wagon trails and at forts. Saloons were where the miners and cowboys would go for entertainment after long days of backbreaking work. These places provided not only whiskey but also gambling such as monte, faro, roulette, twenty-one and poker, as well as female companionship.

The saloons in Brooklyn offered a wide array of entertainment besides alcoholic drinks such as beer and whiskey; there were billiards, cigar rooms,

## The Northwestern Bar

### *The Family Liquor House.*

ONLY THE FINEST BRANDS OF WINES. LIQUORS AND CIGARS CARRIED IN STOCK. ROSEDALE. WHISKEY CAN'T BE BEAT. IN BEERS WE HAVE BUDWEISER, BLUE RIBBON, CHRYSTAL SPRINGS. KEG BEER ON TAP. *SAM PETERSON, Proprietor, Brooklyn.*

The Northwestern Bar, owned by Sam Peterson, brother to saloon man Tom Piercen of Oak Creek. *Colorado Archives.*

live music, occasional boxing matches and, of course, various types of gambling and female companionship. The saloons in Brooklyn didn't adhere to any rules of operations other than closing on Sundays for the Sabbath; day or night, a patron could get a drink or find a game of cards.

A number of different people petitioned for liquor licenses for the Brooklyn side. Some stayed in business for only a short time, pulling up stakes and moving on to more prosperous prospects in the West, while a few others stayed until Prohibition in Colorado put them out of business in 1916. The four most well-known saloon owners were Anton Kline, Gus Durbin, J. "Shorty" Anderson and Lem McAlpine.

## The Deacon: Anton Kline

Anton was generally seen as the "good guy" in Brooklyn due to his close association with the law and his higher standards of saloon operation that included not allowing women or children in his saloon and running fair gambling tables. Kline made the newspaper only once for alleged illegal behavior, unlike many of the other saloon owners. This incident occurred when the railroad first arrived in Steamboat in January 1909. Anton and other saloon owners were chastised by a local minister, a Reverend Evans of the local Congregational church, for allegedly serving alcohol on the Sabbath, which was illegal.[33] This happened to have occurred when the celebrations for the arrival of the long-anticipated Moffat railroad tracks reached Steamboat and the town was celebrating its arrival. The reverend had the sheriff march all the saloon owners to the town side for a hearing on the charges of serving alcohol on the Sabbath. The charges were later dropped due to the nature of the celebrations of the train's arrival to town and Kline's ability to glibly talk his way out of anything. His gift for talk and knowledge of scripture inspired his nickname, the Deacon.[34]

Anton was born in June 1861 in Germany.[35] Rumors abound regarding Anton's hazy past prior to his arrival in Steamboat Springs. He supposedly spent a number of years in various locales such as Johannesburg, South Africa, and Canada, where he supposedly served as an officer of the Canadian Northwest Mounted Police for over twenty-five years. Anton kept his past to himself and intended it to stay that way. According to Anton's descendants, he burned all photos and documents of his early days in a bonfire outside his ranch house in Deep Creek.[36]

# Kline's Capital Bar

## Just a few Blocks from the Bath House.

## All Colorado Beer 25c Bottle
## Budweiser, 3 Bottles for $1

All the leading brands of liquors, such as Old Crow, Taylor, Hermitage and foreign as well as domestic wines. All orders delivered promptly.

**Tel. Mountain 41**                          **A. KLINE, Prop.**

Anton Kline's saloon ad. *Colorado Archives.*

Anton immigrated to the United States in 1875, heading out west and eventually landing in the Southwest.[37] In 1895, he married Miss Clara Meade, and they settled down in the Flagstaff City area in the Arizona Territory.[38] Anton owned a saloon called the Germania, as well as a sheep ranch just outside town.[39] Things went well for the Klines for a number of years until an incident in 1902 caused Anton and his family to abruptly leave the country. The young family went to live in South Africa for a few years. According to family members, Anton had killed a man, and because of the circumstances, instead of jail the family was forced to leave the country. The story goes that Anton was out fixing a fence on his ranch when he fell from his horse and broke his leg. While lying on the ground, unable to get up to find help, as his horse had run off, a man rode up and, although he saw that Anton was in dire distress, did not stop to help him. Anton yelled out to the man that if ever he saw him again, he would kill him for leaving him there. Some years later, Anton ran into the same man, and being a man of his word, he shot him dead.[40] Anton packed up his wife and three young children and boarded a ship to South Africa. The Klines lived in South Africa for a few years before eventually returning to the United States, and by 1908, they were living in Routt County.

Regardless of what his past may have been, as he kept it to himself, Kline was critical of the immoral behavior of some of the other saloon owners. His saloon the Capital was considered a respectable place that did not allow women to enter, and he was known for running clean gambling tables. Even the ladies of town felt that Kline was a respectable businessman, although they did not necessarily approve of his profession: "We women are opposed to all saloon licenses, but if the town must have a saloon in order to raise revenue then Mr. Kline should have the sole right and the rest of them should be cut out."[41]

Kline's higher standard of ethics in no way meant that he was not up to the rough ways of the West; he could hold his own in the rowdy company of the saloon business, as illustrated by a story told by his son, Anton Jr., in an interview in the spring 1982 issue of the *Three Wire Winter* magazine:

> *There were a bunch of hard rockers that was putting that cut in there by where the depot is. At that time this hard rocker come up there, and he was a Swede. As he held my dad up, I was standing by the end of the bar. Me and my brother always had to clean the saloon in the evening, see. "So alright," my dad says, "safe's open." Well the robber got the money sack and he came by the drawers and got all the cash out of them and walked over to the door…Well when that man went to the door, and where my dad got that gun, I don't know, but Dad hit him and that gun and sack fell on the ground. He [Dad] said "now get out of here and don't come back."*[42]

Kline and the local sheriff at the time, Charley Neiman, were the best of friends, and they were known to hang out in the back of Kline's saloon playing cards with their .45s. Kline was concerned with the moral and social conditions in Brooklyn and constantly protested the sketchy goings-on at other establishments in Brooklyn, but to no avail. Eventually, he got tired of the business and took up ranching. Anton sold his saloon in 1912 to a Fred McKay from Utah and moved his family to a ranch in the Deep Creek area of Routt County.[43]

# GUS DURBIN

Augustine "Gus" Durbin was born in Kentucky in 1869.[44] It is unknown when the entrepreneurial Gus arrived in Steamboat; the earliest he appears in local records is in 1903, when he is mentioned in the newspaper as opening the Waunita Bar in Brooklyn, which he later sold to Anton Kline. In 1905, Durbin opened a temperance saloon on the city side of the river.[45] He seemed

Carrie Nation saloon ad. *Colorado Archives.*

to have a considerable sense of humor and named his temperance saloon the
Carrie Nation, after the notorious Carrie Nation, a fiery temperance leader
of the period who was known for her radical attacks on saloons, where she
would use her hatchet to break open barrels of booze. Durbin later moved
this saloon to the Brooklyn side of the river and petitioned for a liquor license
while still maintaining the same business name. In 1906, he married a Mrs.
Nellie Finley in Carbon, Wyoming.[46] Nellie, who had recently divorced, was
a local young lady who was running a boardinghouse and restaurant on the
main side of town. Gus and Nellie had one child, a girl, in 1907.[47]

Durbin was an entrepreneurial type who invested in a number of ventures
over the years, including restaurants, other saloons such as the Oasis and
the Manhattan, hotels such as the Brooklyn Hotel and the local limekiln.
He had interests in saloons in Yampa and Oak Creek and attempted to
establish a saloon in the little hamlet of Sidney. Durbin also invested in a
number of placer mines as well as horses, owning one of the local rodeo
favorites, Carrie Nation. He even purchased from an H.E. Burgess in 1909
the Central Stable, which he used to provide a livery service to his Brooklyn
businesses and offered delivery service across the bridge to Steamboat.[48]

One of Durbin's favorite purchases was a Black Maria wagon that he
bought in Denver. For a time, he used this wagon as a means of advertisement
and to gather patrons for his saloon. Deemed the "Booze Wagon" by locals, it
would make its rounds through the town of Steamboat picking up customers
to take over the bridge to Durbin's saloon in Brooklyn.[49] On one occasion,
the wagon picked up an unsuspecting passenger, a well-known politician
from Hahn's Peak. The unnamed gentleman was unaware of the stir he

Carrie Nation ad. *Colorado Archives.*

caused by riding the wagon. He had happily accepted the ride from the wagon's driver, George Palmer, as he had grown tired of walking during the heat of the day. The politician was quite pleased with himself for getting a free tour of the cityscape and thought his popularity had grown such that people kept pointing and waving to him; he heartily returned their waves and smiles. It wasn't until the wagon reached its destination at the Carrie Nation Saloon across the bridge that he realized his error and shamefacedly had to walk back over the bridge.[50]

Gus was actively involved in the community and local politics. He served on the finance committee for the Fourth of July festivities for a number of years and helped organize the Pioneer Days celebration.[51] He served as a trustee to the 1912 County Convention, undoubtedly against prohibition sentiment.[52] He was also a member of the local fraternity called the Grand Aerie Eagles, a "fraternal order of good things," and served as its president in 1908.[53] Gus helped organize the fire department in Brooklyn and donated the use of his fastest team of horses and his Black Maria wagon to serve as the fire hose.[54]

Durbin, however, had a dark side and was associated on a business level with Ollie Patterson's boardinghouse, a known house of ill fame. He was arrested and fined on a number of occasions for running a bawdyhouse, but no major charges ever evolved.

Durbin's lifestyle seemed to have affected his marriage, which ended in a nasty divorce in 1914.[55] Durbin's ex-wife moved to Oak Creek, where she opened a boardinghouse and restaurant and eventually remarried, while

Durbin continued his saloon lifestyle in Brooklyn. Durbin stayed in business until the very end, knowing that prohibition was coming to Colorado on January 1, 1916. According to local historian and author Jean Wren, Durbin was noted as hanging a sign in his saloon stating, "The first of January will be the last of August."[56] Colorado would officially become a dry state at that time, and all saloons would be closed mandatorily.

Gus moved on after prohibition, heading to California near Los Angeles, where his brother, Colonel Durbin, who was an old friend of Buffalo Bill, ran a famous stock farm called the Vindicator.[57] Gus remarried and divorced and even spent some time in jail in California from 1935 to the early 1940s.[58] Eventually, he died in Riverside, California, in January 1942.[59] His notorious saloon in Brooklyn, considered among the most popular resorts in northwestern Colorado, later served as a movie setting in an Art-o-Graf film, *The Wolves of Wall Street*. The building was eventually torn down in the 1920s.[60]

# John "Shorty" Anderson

John S. Anderson was better known as "Shorty" Anderson to the people of Steamboat. Originally from Battle Lake, Shorty was another entrepreneur who flocked to Steamboat when news of the Moffat Road railroad construction began to circulate throughout Colorado. In 1908, Shorty purchased two lots in Brooklyn for $800, and in 1909, he built a saloon on one of the lots on the corner opposite Gus Durbin's Carrie Nation Saloon.[61]

Shorty opened two saloons over the course of his time in Steamboat. The first saloon he built was the Mint Saloon, followed by the Antlers Saloon, both in Steamboat Springs. These were common names for saloons, as there were a number of saloons with each name, such as the ones in Yampa that were owned by different people. Like his friend Gus Durbin, Shorty had numerous businesses ventures, including interests in mining claims in the Blue Mountains, interest in the local limekiln and a business relationship with a local notorious boardinghouse madam by the name of Hazel McGuire. Shorty also participated in helping organize town events such as the Fourth of July celebration in 1913, of which he served as the president of the festivities committee.[62]

Shorty, however, was not as fortunate as some of the other saloon owners when it came to avoiding trouble with the law. On a number of occasions,

Shorty was brought up on some serious charges, including being fined. In August 1914, aware of impending charges of white slavery, Shorty abruptly left town. Later that month, he was arrested in Baggs, Wyoming, and charged with the white slavery offense in addition to assisting in the maintenance of a house of prostitution.[63] These charges were eventually dropped in 1916, but they weren't his only woes. The Antlers Saloon in Brooklyn burned down along with his residence in November 1914.[64] Anderson supposedly lost up to $10,000 of property, for which he stated he was only insured for $4,000. The fire raised suspicions when it was discovered that it had started in the residence, in which no one had stayed for a few days. Shorty had also taken up a lease in Craig on the Manhattan Hotel and Bar in October 1914. The Manhattan also mysteriously burned down the following year in November 1915.[65] Arson was suspected in the latter fire; however, no charges were ever filed. Shorty and his wife moved to Denver shortly after the Manhattan fire in December 1915.

Shorty later returned to Steamboat Springs after prohibition took hold, but his interests were no longer in the saloon business; instead, he was focused on the lime industry. Lime was a key ingredient in a number of building products, especially plaster for interior walls. This made it a profitable investment in growing towns. Shorty led a fairly quiet life after the saloons closed, staying out of the newspaper spotlight until he dropped dead of heart disease in February 1928 in Pershing, Colorado, near a lime claim he owned that he was checking on.[66]

# LEM MCALPINE

Lemuel Dennis McAlpine was born on October 28, 1860, in Nova Scotia, Canada.[67] He immigrated to the United States sometime in 1879 and first shows up in Routt County records in 1900, living in Hayden, Colorado, in a tent home with his wife, Selma, and her parents while working as a teamster.[68] By 1906, he had partnered with a man by the name of Zick to operate the National Sawmill, a flourishing business with all the construction going on.[69] That same year, he also purchased the Onyx Hotel on the Steamboat proper side for his wife to run. Lemuel, or "Lem," as he was called, helped manage Gus Durbin's saloon in Brooklyn during the winter months of 1911 while the lumber mill was down for the season. He must have seen the possibilities of making large amounts of money in the saloon business because by 1913 he started purchasing interests in various saloons across Routt County, including Brooklyn, Phippsburg and, later, Oak Creek.

Although Lem was never very politically active, he did vocalize a protest regarding the treatment of Brooklyn people by the local Steamboat Bath House management. The incident arose in March 1911 while Lem was managing Gus Durbin's saloon the Carrie Nation. Since there was little to no indoor plumbing, many area residents took their winter baths at the local hot springs bathhouse, which was located on the town side of the river just over the bridge from Brooklyn. The costs of the baths were generally about $0.50 per person at that time of year. However, four women from Brooklyn—it's unknown whether they were prostitutes—went for a bath and were charged $13.30 each.[70] McAlpine saw this as unfair to the population of Brooklyn, which consisted of not only saloon people but also immigrants and new arrivals to town, and brought the incident to the public's awareness at a meeting held in Brooklyn at the Carrie Nation Saloon. The residents of Brooklyn were outraged at the obvious slight, and the matter made the local newspapers as a possible item for the next town meeting. However, the Brooklyn group was late in putting the issue on the agenda, and nothing was mentioned further.

Besides being the owner of a sawmill and different saloons, Lem was also a well-known heavyweight prizefighter and participated in a few large prizefights in Routt County. The first of these was in 1907, when he fought "Happy Hooligan Small" of Yampa for six rounds.[71] One of his most publicized fights was with Charley Williams from the Little Snake area in 1905.[72] The fight garnered over $180 in gate fees and attracted numbers of people from all over Northwest Colorado and the Little Snake River area of southern Wyoming. McAlpine, at forty-six years old, was the favorite. Although he was quite a bit older than Williams, he was the seasoned veteran fighter. The match lasted thirteen exciting rounds, finally ending with Williams winning. It was speculated that McAlpine might have won the bout if he had not broken his hand in the first few rounds, putting him off his game.[73]

McAlpine and his wife finally had a child, a son, in 1914, which caused Lem to look for opportunities elsewhere. Lem bounced about the county with his saloon investments while continuing to operate his sawmill operation, occasionally working for the Sarvis Lumber Company and all the while making trips to Oregon to check on sawmill opportunities there. In 1915, Lem and his wife started selling off their property, and in 1917, they relocated with their young son to Oregon, where Lem found work as a sawmill operator.

# Chapter 6

# THE INMATES OF BROOKLYN

W estern expansion offered ample opportunities for single men to make their fortunes in the form of backbreaking physical labor in industries such as lumberjacking, mining, moving freight, railroad construction and cattle driving. This created not only a male-dominant workforce but also a predominately male society on the frontier. Hard conditions of the frontier—such as the long and difficult journey westward; constant threats of Indian hostility; primitive, substandard living conditions; and few economic opportunities—attracted very few women and families to the West. Most jobs were held by men; the few respectable jobs open to women were few and far between and paid very little. Most respectable jobs, such as clerical positions, were usually filled by males or relatives of owners. The only job opportunities that were left for women on the frontier, beyond marriage, included work as laundresses, cooks, dressmakers, milliners, waitresses and actresses. These jobs required little to no skills and attracted women who were unskilled and uneducated. In turn, they paid minimal wages. Although some of these services were heavily used and needed on the frontier, the work was hard and labor intensive, and these jobs lacked any social respectability of the period because these women were considered poor. Later on, as some families moved westward, economic opportunities in the form of teaching positions arose for young, single women who had some education. However, these were very limited and confining, especially in the restrictions placed on the teachers themselves by local school boards, and averaged only a paltry annual income between $285 and $450 in 1900.[74] Although some women did prosper under respectable means, the largest employment or economic opportunity for women came in the form of prostitution.

Although muddled through the passage of time, the vision of the prostitute as some icon of female independence and social radicalism is a product of modern entertainment. There were many reasons women took to prostitution, but the majority of those reasons were economically motivated. This was a time when there were no social services to aid women whose husbands had died or deserted them. Many young women resorted to the only means of making money other than remarriage: the oldest profession of prostitution. Respectable jobs, such as restaurant work, store clerk or factory work, required ten-hour workdays and offered very little pay. A clerk who worked from sunup to sundown six days a week averaged about $6 per week, while rent in a cheap place was about $4 per week, leaving little for food and other expenses, let alone supporting a family or getting ahead.[75] A lowly prostitute in the same town averaged about $10 to $20 per week and in boomtowns anywhere from $40 to $175 per week.[76] Women who became prostitutes came from various backgrounds and racial heritages and worked in different types of situations that varied greatly. Some girls worked in fancy brothels wearing fine clothes with servants to wait on them and a madam

Second Street Bridge with Brooklyn in background, 1908. *Tread of Pioneers Museum.*

Looking up the Yampa River toward where the original Second Street Bridge stood. *Author's collection.*

to watch over them. Others plied their wares from their doorways in small row houses called cribs; still others worked independently out of their own cabins or cottages, while the lowest were relegated to working as common streetwalkers, selling themselves for whiskey in back alleys.[77]

In Steamboat's Brooklyn, prostitution took two dominant forms: cabins and rooming house brothels. The cabins, which were more like small shacks, lined the narrow streets of the small neighborhood of Brooklyn next to the railroad tracks. According to local historian Jean Wren, these ladies would put their lamps on outside their shacks to let their customers know they were ready to entertain. Very little is known of these women, as they stayed only briefly, keeping ahead of the law. Most of the young ladies resided in the rooming house brothels and were brought in from other locales such as Denver. Some were moved along the railroad survey by the saloon owners making the sweep through Northwest Colorado to Craig only to continue to Rock Springs, Wyoming, and other parts of the West. These women met their potential customers at the saloons and took them back to their rooms to entertain them.

There were two leading brothels in Brooklyn that were noted as being "rooming houses"; one was run by Ollie Patterson and the other by Hazel McGuire.

# Ollie Patterson

Ollie was born Iva Ethel Griffin on May 12, 1874, in Muskegan, Michigan.[78] In 1879, her family moved to Trinidad, Colorado, where her father, Henry Griffin, worked as a master mechanic for the Victor Fuel Company. Two more siblings were born after their arrival in Colorado. Around 1891, Iva married a man named MacQuarrie who came from Canada, and they had two children: a son named Rowland, born in 1892, and a daughter named Clara, born in 1894. In late 1902, Iva's mother passed away after a brief illness, and her father, distraught over her death, moved in with her. Iva's husband most likely died or abandoned her about this same time, as he does not appear in any records. Iva's two children went to live with her married sister in Hastings, Colorado, while Iva and her father moved to Steamboat Springs.

Once in Steamboat Springs, Iva purchased two Brooklyn lots from W.E. Harris for $300 in March 1905 under the name of Ollie Patterson.[79] Oddly enough, this was the name of an infamous Leadville madam who had been killed a few years earlier in 1892.[80] Iva, or Ollie now, apparently never entertained men in her boardinghouse but rather boarded young "married" women who plied their wares at Durbin's saloon. Although Ollie had a notorious reputation, she never ran into trouble with the authorities, and it was Durbin instead who faced fines on a few occasions for white slavery for having the girls prostituting in his saloon.

In December 1909, a fire on the third floor of Ollie's rooming house threatened to burn her out of business.[81] In a time when fires usually destroyed entire buildings and blocks, Ollie was quite fortunate. The newly implemented town fire alarm sounded, and the fire crew was astonishingly quick in getting to her establishment and putting out the flames. Afterward, Ollie called Gus to set up free rounds of drinks for the boys at his bar that they were likewise quick to dispose of.

Things were going quite well financially for Ollie, and by 1910, she was able to place her daughter in a private boarding school, the Loretta Academy in Pueblo, Colorado. This was far from Ollie's socially unaccepted business, which kept Clara safe from any gossip. Her son, Rowland, was grown by now and worked for the railroad while living in Denver. Ollie was noted for making frequent trips to Denver over the years. Whether these trips were business trips to find new girls for her rooming house or to visit her children is not known. According to the 1910 census, Ollie considered herself the head of household, owning her own rooming house, yet she was "married" to a William Patterson, a carpenter who was twenty years her senior. Ollie was doing quite well for herself, even having a servant, a widow named Naomi Kelly. Ollie had a number of young "married" roomers whose husbands were not with them at her establishment.[82] She listed four young women for the 1910 census. According to Marcellus Merrill, a longtime Steamboat resident, "Every Saturday afternoon, Ollie Patterson, who ran a sporting house of ill fame in Brooklyn, would parade down Main Street with several of her best looking gals dressed up 'fit to kill,' trying to attract a little business from some of the cowpunchers."[83]

In April 1919, Ollie was quite wealthy, owning "considerable property in Brooklyn," and was going by the name of Ethel Macquarrie when she married Lige Merrit, who worked at the nearby lumber mill. Ollie lived respectably and comfortably, buying touring cars for both her husband and herself and traveling with her husband, who worked for various mines. She even invested in a few mining ventures. The Merrits were living in the town of Mount Harris when Ollie took ill rather suddenly and was admitted to the Hayden Solandt Hospital. Her grown daughter and son, as well as her sister, stayed with her while she was in the hospital, along with her husband, and they were all at her bedside when she passed away in 1927 from Bright's disease.[84] Her husband, Lige, was lost after her sudden death and passed away just a few months later, leaving a considerable estate that Ollie had amassed, including a number of properties in the Brooklyn neighborhood of Steamboat. Ollie and Lige were buried beside each other in the Steamboat Springs Cemetery, their graves marked with a single marble headstone that has disappeared over time.

# HAZEL MCGUIRE

The Mint Saloon, owned by J.F. "Shorty" Anderson, was notorious for having a "rooming house" built onto the rear of the saloon. This rooming house was run by another infamous lady by the name of Hazel McGuire. According to the 1910 census, Hazel was born in New Hampshire in 1876.[85] It was believed that Hazel was brought to Steamboat from Oak Creek by one of her regular boarders, a cowboy by the name of Andy Black. Andy worked as a bartender in one of the saloons and occasionally competed in the rodeo. He seemed to be quite a ladies' man and a bit of a rake, causing quite a stir with the "respectable" people of Steamboat Springs when he would parade a different one of Hazel's girls as his "wife" at each rodeo event.[86] Andy purchased a succession of ranches in South Routt and eventually settled down in Yampa with a local girl.

Hazel was considered to have one of the leading parlor houses for a time. Like Ollie, Hazel listed only two "roomers" when the federal census was compiled in 1910.[87] Both of these "roomers" were young and supposedly married, although no husbands were listed as living with them. One of Hazel's roomers in 1910 was a Louise Wheeler and the other a young Nellie Smith from Rawlins, Wyoming.[88] Nellie Smith, or Lil' Nelle, her working nickname, apparently was not happy with her situation and had attempted to commit suicide by drinking a "large dose of corrosive sublimate" in November 1909.[89] Prostitutes commonly drank poison or overdosed on drugs such as laudanum as a means of suicide. Nellie, however, survived the attempt due to the local doctor's quick response and was still in residence at Hazel McGuire's establishment over a year later.

Despite the popularity of Hazel's parlor house, she eventually sold her property to Andy Black in 1912 for $300.[90] Why Hazel decided to sell her property is somewhat speculative; however, it seems that Hazel was having a run of bad luck. In the summer of 1911, Hazel, three men (including Andy Black) and two other "inmates" from Brooklyn ran afoul of the authorities and were facing jail time in a federal penitentiary. Oddly, the crime had nothing to do with prostitution but was a violation of game and fish laws. Hazel, along with the others, was arrested for dynamiting fish in Luna Lake, which was located in the newly formed Routt National Forest.[91] Charges were later mysteriously dropped against Hazel, Andy and the other two women; however, the other two men were found guilty and sent to prison. Hazel would be at the front of another public scandal the following March. It seems that a young married woman from Oak Creek had been forced by necessity, according to the newspapers, to become an inmate at Hazel's establishment after her husband had been sent to the county jail for theft. Once her husband was released, he found his wife "working" in Hazel's brothel and was so distraught at what she had been doing that he attempted to shoot himself in her room.[92]

Whatever the cause, Hazel sold out two months later and disappeared from Steamboat Springs. Rumors abounded that she had disappeared to Rock Springs, Wyoming, a favorite place for her business partner, Shorty Anderson, to go. According to a newspaper article in the *Routt County Sentinel*, Hazel died in November 1914 "in a poor farm in Wyoming, as an insane patient." Hazel did, in fact, pass away on November 5, 1914, at the Wyoming State Hospital for the Insane in Evanston, Wyoming, where she had been committed since December 1913. Her death certificate was vague on the cause of death listing.[93] Hazel most likely had contracted a venereal disease such as syphilis from her profession, which was a common affliction of prostitutes that in its later stages leads to insanity and death. Hazel was buried in the hospital cemetery with no known relatives attending; she was only thirty-eight years old.

# THE UNKNOWNS

There were other houses of ill repute in Brooklyn, but Ollie's and Hazel's were the dominant ones. There were other girls in Brooklyn who worked out of the small shanty houses that dotted the Brooklyn neighborhood. These unknowns composed a huge percentage of the young women who moved about from town to town in the West. Rarely did a prostitute use her real name or stay in one place too long, as it was bad for business. Girls moved about frequently in order to maintain an interested clientele and make as much money as possible.

Sometimes, girls would form relationships that would cause them problems, as was the case with Miss Georgia Woods, whose lover committed suicide in nearby Oak Creek. Other girls managed to marry and settle down, leaving their old lives behind them, although a few failed to take to the constraints of being wives. One popular Brooklyn young lady, a Lou MacQuistern, married a cowboy from Maybell in 1910. According to the newspaper announcement, the judge performing the service opted not to kiss the bride, as was customary at the wedding in this case.[94] This marriage was short-lived, and in 1913, the young husband filed for divorce based on his wife's drunkenness; the divorce went uncontested.[95]

Then there were girls such Margaret Roe, Mary Doe and Lil' Nell, who left no trace other than their names on the 1910 census or in newspaper articles as all that remains as a testament that they even existed. When a prostitute died, she was placed in the lower section of the cemetery, commonly referred to as Potters Field, where those who were destitute or vagrant were buried, with just a wooden cross if any to mark her place. These women were shadows in society in life and even in death. Eventually, their notoriety and names faded into history.

# Chapter 7
# STORIES OF BROOKLYN

## Confrontation in Routt National Forest

Shorty Anderson and Hazel McGuire were not the only people to run afoul of the authorities. An entrepreneurial saloonkeeper by the name of Oscar Walker, who worked in Brooklyn as a bartender for a time, received a liquor license from the county commissioners in the spring of 1909 to operate a saloon in Columbine. Walker went to Steamboat Springs, loaded up a wagon full of whiskey, gathered three working girls from one of the rooming houses in Brooklyn and hauled them up to the first sheep camp roundups in the Routt National Forest to make some easy money during the summer of 1909.[96] The report given by Ranger Ray Peck stated that the girls and whiskey caused quite a distraction for the sheepherders, who subsequently left their flocks unattended; eleven bands of ewes and lambs were mixed up as a result. It required the construction of corrals to separate the sheep. The corrals took days to construct and more days to round the sheep back up and separate out the different bands, which put an unanticipated delay on the trail schedule and irritated the forest supervisor. According to Ranger Peck, his supervisor, Mr. Ratliff, made sure that the girls would never return to the forest during a roundup again. Supposedly, he tied the leader of the Brooklyn girls to a tree and threatened to leave her there unless she promised to take the other girls, leave the country and never return. When she finally agreed, he lopped off a chunk of her hair before untying her. He allegedly kept the girl's hair as a memento, tying it with a ribbon, and hung it in the

Whiskey Park Ranger Station, where it remained for many years until the station burned down.[97] Nothing more was said of Mr. Walker, who seemed to have left the scene of the incident unscathed.

## OUTLAWS IN BROOKLYN

Brooklyn was supposedly also a favorite hangout for gunslingers and outlaws such as the Browns Park legendary Butch Cassidy and the Hole in the Wall Gang. Although other towns had saloons and ladies of tarnished reputations, Brooklyn had a number of saloons with back rooms in which a person of notoriety could go unnoticed. According to a local legend, Cassidy and his outlaw associates held a parlay in Brooklyn to decide if they wanted to hang up their spurs and enlist in the Spanish-American War. Apparently, the outcome of the vote was no, and they continued their outlaw ways.[98]

## SHOOTOUTS

No picture of a saloon district would be complete without some form of a shootout. Brooklyn was not a terribly violent red-light district when compared to some of the other western towns in America, but it did have a few stories of violence. One such incident occurred in June 1908. Apparently, about 3:00 a.m. one Wednesday morning, Doc Floyd, a local merchant, got angry after a card game of draw and pulled a gun on Dick Gorden, the night cook at the Caraway Restaurant that was attached to the back of Gus Durbin's saloon.[99] Four shots were fired by Doc Floyd. The first shot hit Gorden in the muscle of his arm. Gorden ran at Doc Floyd to try to disarm him before he could get off another shot. While the two men wrestled for the gun, a number of shots went off, the first hitting Gorden in the small of his back. The third and fourth shot fired by Doc while the men continued to fight over the gun hit Doc himself, once through the hand and another in the shoulder.[100] It appeared that charges were pending; however, both victims had to recuperate before anything was filed.

Brooklyn would make the front page for another saloon shooting. In September 1909, W.G. Williams, a Texas cowboy locally known as "Tex," had been drinking heavily in the rear of Shorty Anderson's saloon. He started playing with his gun in a drunken attempt to show off his pistol skills and accidentally shot himself in the leg. The wound proved to be a fatal one, as Tex bled to death before a doctor could be summoned to look at the injury.[101]

# THE GOLDEN HEN

Not all the stories of Brooklyn centered on the saloon gang, as they were known. There were also families who lived on the Brooklyn side of the river, and one of these was the Garten family. The elder Garten held quite a bit of respectability with the Brooklyn crowd, as he was nominated as a mayoral candidate and often referred to as the "mayor of Brooklyn," although he doesn't appear to have been in the saloon business. It seems that the Gartens kept chickens on their property, which was common for both eggs and poultry. One Saturday afternoon, Mr. Garten picked out a fat hen for Sunday dinner. After he had killed the chicken, he promptly gave it to his daughter to pluck, clean and dress. While the young lady was cleaning the chicken, she discovered a large nugget of gold that the hen had apparently eaten. This caused quite a stir in Brooklyn, and numerous theories as to where the large nugget came from emerged, which started a small rush onto the hillside from which the gold might have washed down. Mr. Garten apparently thought that he would find a large placer lode on his property; however, no other nuggets were ever discovered.[102]

Part III

# Gateway to the Flattops and Routt County

# Chapter 8

# YAMPA

Long before Yampa was assured its spot on the Moffat Railroad main line through Northwest Colorado, the area boomed with cattle and agricultural production and served as a stage stop. The town started to take form about 1884, budding from a small colony of ranches that were situated close together. These ranches included those of Sam C. Reid, George Crossan, Edwin McFarland and Preston King, to name just a few.[103] Samuel Fix is noted as the first white person to settle in the area of Yampa in the very early years of 1880, with numerous families entering the area in the mid- to late 1880s.[104] In 1886, Henry Hernage started a small store where the present town of Yampa is located, and a man by the name of William Rockhill, who came in the early 1880s to ranch, also established a saloon business.[105] With the development of the stage road through Gore Canyon, the area became a natural stopping point for travelers en route to other points in Northwest Colorado. The hamlet was known only as Egeria in these early days, since it was the largest settlement situated in the lower Egeria Park area. Sometime around 1892, Ira Van Camp established a stage stop nearby on his ranch that marked the eastern border of the small village.[106] Rancher George Crossan, who was also a carpenter, opened a store and built a number of small cabins in the little colony and tried to induce people to come to the area. The post office was established in 1894, and on the application, there were two names submitted: Yampa or Hernageville.[107] The name Yampa won out, and from then on, the town was known as Yampa.

The small village of Yampa grew steadily, as it was the gateway town to the rest of Routt County, being situated in the southern part of the Yampa

Valley just north of the Gore Pass, which connected the valley to Hot Sulphur Springs and Kremmling to the east. It was also on the route to the nearest train terminal to the south at Wolcott. Travelers and cattlemen had to pass through Yampa either en route to deliver their goods and cattle to the shipping point at Walcott or to get to the northern areas of Routt County.

Other businesses quickly followed the establishment of the post office, and by 1903, the town boasted in the newly launched local newspaper, the *Yampa Leader*, of having four general merchandise stores, one grocery store, one drugstore, two first-class hotels, two livery stables, two blacksmith shops, one millinery and dressmaking parlor, one laundry, two butchers, one newspaper, one bank, one church, one school, three real estate offices and two saloons, to name just a few of the amenities of the growing town.[108] Ads such as the following, from a June 13, 1903 supplemental, were constantly in the *Yampa Leader*: "Don't let the grass grow under your feet about getting to Yampa. Pull up stakes ye weary eastern pilgrim, and come runnin'. We have plenty of room for sober industrious citizens."[109]

Crews of railroad surveyors and graders began to descend on the area in 1904, boosting the population and town growth. With the prospects of the Moffat line directly going through Yampa and the hope of a Union Station on the eastern side of town, the town was a sure bet for any entrepreneurial-minded individuals. The town was not incorporated until 1906, when many of the citizens felt that monies paid for licenses such as for saloons, drugstores, grocers and dogs should go to their own town's improvements rather than to the county treasury. After the town incorporated, Ordinance No. 6 set saloon fees at $500 per year, which added to the town's municipal treasury.[110] The first train finally arrived on September 18, 1908, connecting the area to Denver markets and allowing more crops and livestock to be shipped, as well as affording tourism. For a brief time, the town boomed as a shipping center as well as a tourist haven, being hailed as a sporting paradise for hunters and fishermen who came to the area to visit Trapper Lake and the Flattops area.

Yampa boasted only a few saloons in its heyday, including the Turf Saloon, the Mint Saloon and, later, the Antlers Bar and Tom Piercen's Northwestern Saloon, which was open for only about a year. The saloons were located on one of the town's main thoroughfares called Moffat Avenue, which was its main business district. Rarely were Yampa saloons mentioned for disorderly behavior, although things must have been getting a bit tense in 1908 when a special town meeting was held in February regarding the gambling that was going on in the saloons. The town adopted the following motion: "The marshal is hereby instructed to notify all saloons and other public places

The Wolcott Stage, circa 1905. *Hayden Heritage Center.*

The Antlers in Yampa, 1907. *Courtesy Rita Herold Collection.*

that all gambling must stop at once, and to arrest any and all persons found engaged in gambling; also to arrest the owners or tenants of places where gambling is allowed."[111]

The only other event that occurred in the saloons was the sudden death of Pieder Gunderson, a Norwegian laborer, who dropped dead in the Mint Saloon one evening, apparently from chronic alcoholism.[112] The saloon business didn't seem to thrive in the small town that was quickly becoming family friendly. In 1909, Piercen moved his saloon and fixtures of the Northwestern to Oak Creek.[113] Earlier that same year, Marcus Hight and George A. Moore had moved their saloon, the Mint, to Brooklyn outside Steamboat Springs.[114] By 1913, the town only had one saloon, the Antlers bar, and the citizens and town trustees seemed quite content with that number and raised the saloon fee to $1,000 per year to make up the difference.[115]

There were also hotels such as the Antlers Hotel, the Monte Cristo and the Royal Hotel. The Antlers was one of the first hotels built by Thomas P. Lindsay in 1902.[116] He later built another hotel, in 1906, on Moffat Avenue for a Mr. and Mrs. Greer, who promptly sold it to a Mrs. Strine, who named it the Royal Hotel.[117] The Royal was one of the largest hotels in Routt County until the Cabin Hotel was built in Steamboat Springs. According to the authors of *The Historical Guide to Routt County*, there were a few shacks or cribs behind the Antlers bar that housed the town's few soiled doves during the early days of the construction of the railroad. The construction of the railroad consisted of large numbers of hardworking crews, from graders to track layers, who looked for some relaxation during any off hours before they moved on toward the Oak Creek area and then on to Steamboat.[118]

The Royal Hotel on Moffat Avenue in Yampa. *Author's collection.*

A saloon painting hanging in the Antlers Café in Yampa, Colorado. This painting originally hung in one of the saloons in Oak Creek. *Author's photo, courtesy Antlers Café.*

Yampa was also on the cattle trail in the early days, and although many cattle towns had a few ladies of the evening to accommodate the boisterous cowboys who came through their towns, if Yampa did it would have been for a very brief period, as the town was very family oriented. Behavior such as this was ousted to the outskirts of the area, to ranch saloons. It was during this early period of Yampa history, when it was still regarded as Egeria, that the notorious Ward family came to settle in the area and set up a notorious rest stop for travelers before being forced to relocate to a site several miles south of the town of Lay in the western part of the county.

# Chapter 9
# THE WARD FAMILY

The Ward family—which consisted of Joe Ward; his wife, Harriet; and two children, Etta and Clovis—came to Routt County sometime around 1882.[119] Joe and Harriet, or "Hattie" as she was called, originally hailed from Ohio, where Joe was born in 1834.[120] Joe and Hattie moved westward in the 1870s, making their way to Colorado Springs, where they opened what was considered a "low dive" drinking establishment.[121] It was there in 1879 that Joe ran into trouble with the authorities; however, according to some, it was his second run-in with the law. According to an account in the newspaper, Joe had killed a man in the Black Hills area before he came to Colorado, although no documentation that corroborates that accusation could be found. Regardless, Joe and Hattie were running a saloon of sorts when three young men who had been drinking throughout town all evening tried to gain admittance to their establishment and were refused. Angry that Joe would not let them in, one of the men picked up a stool from the porch and threw it at the door, breaking out a panel. Joe quickly opened the door and, without hesitating, fired his rifle, instantly killing a man by the name of Schiedler.[122] Ward was supposedly sentenced to the state penitentiary for two years on the general principle of being so quick to shoot. According to records, there was a Joe Ward sentenced at that time for larceny.[123]

After Joe was released from prison, he and his family moved about Colorado, living in Leadville and Salida before finally moving to Egeria Park, to the area now known as Yampa.[124] The family lived in town, setting up a roadhouse restaurant saloon for travelers on the river near the present-day site of Yampa.

Possibly the infamous Joe Ward 1880 mug shot from the Colorado Territorial Prison. *Colorado Archives.*

At this time in 1883, the area was along the Trough Road, which was the popular route of the stage, freight wagons and cowboys going to and from Northwest Colorado to the nearest railroad station at Wolcott, which made the Ward establishment a popular watering hole. In addition to the ranch saloon, it was rumored that Joe cattle-rustled and occasionally ran freight with a man named Charley Fox, a local cowboy. Charley became a bit too intimate with Joe's wife one evening, so Joe shot him in the head with his Winchester, killing him instantly.[125]

Ward fled the area, and the townspeople forced the rest of the family to leave, as they felt that the women's morals were too loose. Hat and her teenage children Etta and Clovis packed their belongings and headed west, setting up another roadhouse on the Yampa River. This one was located near the first government bridge built across the river in what is now Moffat County on the Rawlins to Meeker stage line, seven miles southwest of Lay near Juniper.[126] According to the 1885 census taken in June, Hat Ward was married, but her husband, Joe, was not living with her. Along with her two teenage children, she had several male boarders. Business was good enough that Hat owned the house and property.

It was around this time that Joe Ward was gunned down just south of Dixon, Wyoming, where his body was found on July 4, 1885, along the stage road.[127] It was apparent that he had been recently shot eight times and left for dead. According to the *Cheyenne Daily Sun*, his assailants were a posse of Bear River residents who called themselves a "committee of public safety" who were bent on getting Joe to leave the state for good.[128] Other stories concluded that possibly Joe's cattle-rustling companions had killed him; regardless, Joe's reputation as a bad man left the possibilities wide open, and little time or effort was expended on trying to find his killer.

Old Hat, as Hattie was sometimes referred to, and her grown children, Etta and Clovis, maintained the ranch saloon. The place was already a popular stopping spot with the cowboys and was known for its all-night orgies. Sometime in the early 1890s, Etta moved to the booming town of Rico, Colorado, and it was here in 1893 that, for some reason, whether over despair of her life or loss of a love, she drank poison and committed suicide.[129] This left Old Hat and her son Clovis, who was considered to be somewhat slow in the head, to carry on the business.

Tragedy seemed to find the Wards, and in May 1900, it struck again. Clovis was intrigued with a bicycle that a cowboy had left outside the saloon one day. Bicycles were a popular new fad throughout the country, and Clovis wanted to try out the newfangled device. He attempted to ride the bike over the wooden bridge when, in a freak accident, a loose plank fell out from under him, and both he and the bike tumbled into the rushing springtime waters. He drowned at the age of thirty-one.[130] Hattie continued to run the saloon alone until the following Christmas Eve, when after a night of revelry with a group of cowboys, she accidentally overturned an oil lamp, starting a fire. Everyone managed to escape the blaze; however, Hattie rushed back into the building to grab some of her belongings. The fire had caught quickly, engulfing the wooden structure, and the roof crashed in on her, killing her.[131] Her death was the tragic end to the Ward family in South Routt County.

# Part IV
# YAMPA VALLEY GOLD

# Chapter 10

# OAK CREEK

Ferdinand V. Hayden's geological survey in 1873 implicated that there were large, rich veins of coal deposits in the Northwest Colorado territory. Early homesteaders dug small mines in the hillsides to retrieve coal to fuel their homes for the long, cold winters. These were known as wagon mines since homesteaders would move the coal by wagon. One of the first wagon coal mines in Routt County was opened near the present-day town of Oak Creek by William Mahoney and Henry Meyers in the late 1880s.[132]

Sizeable company coal mines would eventually follow, coming into the area toward the turn of the century. These capital ventures enabled the construction of large mines that could go deeper into the earth, extracting large amounts of coal. Substantial operations such as Sam Perry's successful mine, which opened in 1905, would bring large numbers of workers into the area, creating a need for a town to meet the growing demands of the significant influx of miners and their families.[133]

The large coal deposits in the area prompted three businessmen from Cripple Creek—Sam Bell, John Sharpe and D.C. Williams—to organize the Oak Creek Town Company in 1906.[134] They purchased the Shuster ranch ten miles north of Yampa and proceeded to lay out a town site in 1907.[135] The town quickly incorporated by November 1907, although its incorporation had been briefly delayed by the incorporation of the nearby competitor town of Huggins, located just two miles south toward Yampa, also along the Moffat line survey.[136] The Oak Creek Town Company men objected to the incorporation of Huggins so close to their proposed town site. Huggins already had a store and post office by this time and had just granted a saloon license to William Johnston, who opened his saloon in May 1907. The Oak Creek Town Company, led by Sam Bell, fought the validity of Huggins's incorporation in the courts, protesting not only how the town incorporated but also the legality of allowing the construction of a saloon so close to the rail line. The Oak Creek men eventually won the court case, dooming Huggins to obscurity.[137]

The arrival of the train in 1908 would enable large shipments of coal to be transported with profit for both the mines and the Moffat Railroad. According to the *Historical Guide to Routt County*, by 1910, five mines were operating in the vicinity, with a large number of men from all over the world working them.[138] Large numbers of railroad crew workers also settled into the area, as rail yards were established nearby in Phippsburg. This largely male population ensured that saloons and brothels would be very profitable businesses. That same year, the town trustees passed ordinance No. 33, which limited the number of saloons in Oak Creek to five. More saloons could be added at a rate of one for each additional one thousand residents.[139] The town saw significant growth after the arrival of the railroad, and families started to move into the new town.

All was not well for long. November 1913 to February 1914 marked a period of unrest in Oak Creek. The United Mine Workers of America went on strike across Colorado. Tempers flared between union and nonunion miners, leading local authorities to worry about the tensions erupting into all-out violence in Oak Creek, like similar instances in other parts of the state,

Interior of an Oak Creek saloon. *Tracks and Trails Museum.*

A saloon painting that hung in an Oak Creek Saloon. It currently can be seen at the historic Antlers Café, a lovely bar and restaurant that sits in a section of the original Antlers building in Yampa. *Author's photo, courtesy Antlers Café.*

namely the Ludlow Massacre that occurred in April 1914. Fearful of the strikers after a small riot had taken place in Oak Creek, a group called the Taxpayers League organized, supposedly representing one thousand taxpayers and businessmen in the county. This group sought to rid the area of the agitators and distributed warnings throughout the town. The league put out handbills titled "Our Demands," which demanded that certain agitators leave town. The list of names included saloon men William Doyle, James Ray, D.J. Reidy and Tom Piercen. Members of the league, which supposedly included about seven hundred armed men who were ready to ride to Oak Creek, watched as the listed men left on the morning train the following Saturday. The men rode the train to the next town, where they got off and walked back to Oak Creek. They immediately contacted the United Mine Workers Union, which instructed them to take whatever precautions necessary, including shooting anyone who tried to evict them from their homes. Violence seemed inevitable until the troops arrived and established martial law. This briefly established curfews and closed the saloons while the two sides worked out a truce. Eventually, things quieted down and the town returned to normal.

Oak Creek boasted a number of saloons and rooming houses of ill repute and even a small red-light district called Hickory Flats, a place that came more into prominence after prohibition took hold.

# Chapter 11

# TOM PIERCEN

## BOSS MAN OF OAK CREEK

Tom Piercen was born in Norway on July 26, 1871.[140] He immigrated to the United States when he was just sixteen years old and made his way to Cripple Creek, Colorado. He worked in the mines around Leadville for a few years before he got his start in the saloon business. In 1893, he married his first wife, Louisa M. Keagler, and moved to Kremmling,[141] Colorado, to set up business along the path of the new Moffat Line that was heading to Northwest Colorado. Piercen followed the railroad line, setting up saloons and sawmills along the way. Sawmills were especially profitable ventures in railroad boomtowns for the high demand of lumber for new construction, as well as for railroad contracts for railroad ties and outbuildings. Construction was steady not only for new structures but also for rebuilding structures that had burned down, as fire was a constant threat since most buildings were heated with coal or wood stoves and lit with gas lamps.

Tom first set up business in Yampa, establishing the Northwestern Saloon for about a year until he moved his establishment to Oak Creek. In Oak Creek, Tom built a livery stable and then a saloon on Main Street and operated a successful sawmill operation. Eventually, he built the Piercen Block on Main Street and established himself as a town boss of sorts. He ran his red-light district for a number of years out of this notorious downtown building.

Tom's strong connections to the railroad and mine companies gave him a foot up on some of the other saloon owners, much like a town boss. Tom controlled the underworld of Oak Creek; however, it did not keep him from getting in trouble with the law. In 1910, Tom was arrested for causing "bodily harm" to a bar patron by the name of Highline Shorty. Shorty had apparently fallen asleep at the bar, a habit that greatly irritated Tom. So Tom Piercen and his friend Tom Fitzgerald decided to "hot foot" Shorty: the two proceeded to set fire to Shorty's boot after dousing it with alcohol. The prank got out of hand, and poor Shorty was badly burned.[142]

Piercen was also a scrapper and was constantly in different fights. In 1910, he suffered a broken leg when he got into a scuffle with the town marshal, William Phelps.[143] Then, in 1911, while Tom was trying to eject some rowdy drunken patrons, he ended up fighting with one of the men, whom he wrestled to the floor. While Tom was getting the upper hand on the man he had down on the floor, the drunken man's friend, Jack Mann, came up behind Piercen and slashed him with a knife across his face, slicing through his nose and up through his ear. Piercen had to get twenty-five stitches to sew up the wound, which left a permanent scar.[144] Mann received a stint in the state penitentiary for attempting to kill Piercen.

Piercen's legacy as a town boss continued long after prohibition. Piercen's first wife, Louisa Keagler, passed away on Christmas Day 1928.[145] He then married a known woman from Leadville named Louise, nicknamed "Pee Wee," and moved her and her two adult sons up to Oak Creek. Tom and Pee Wee had a tumultuous relationship that ended with a much-publicized divorce in 1939, when he briskly moved her out of their home and moved her sister in.[146] Tom died in 1945, and his notorious business block was torn down in the late 1960s.[147]

# Chapter 12

# SUICIDE OF A SALOON MAN

Little was known about Albert Severson, a local saloon man who was born sometime around 1866 and had no family that anyone knew of.[148] He followed the construction of the Moffat Road, living and starting businesses at several towns along the way to Routt County, where he relocated from Kremmling to Oak Creek in 1907. By 1908, he was serving as a town trustee for Oak Creek and served on a number of committees when he petitioned for a saloon license, which was granted. He wasn't in business very long before the town council deemed his establishment "disorderly" and revoked his license.[149]

Albert's response was to file a lawsuit declaring that the town trustees had no right to revoke his license since the incorporation of the Town of Oak Creek was invalid, as it had no jurisdiction over his license or any other business in town. In Severson's suit, he alleged that although thirty-six people signed the petition for incorporation, many of the people who signed were not legally qualified to sign.[150] The courts placed an injunction on the town board in which it could do no new business until the mess was cleaned up in county court.

Meanwhile, Albert sold his property in Oak Creek and moved to the Brooklyn area of Steamboat Springs, where he took work as a carpenter. That September, Albert fell off a ladder while working on a building in Brooklyn, seriously injuring his head and back.[151] Albert was laid up for a short time, which is when he may have started a turbulent love affair with a "woman of the half world" of Brooklyn named Georgia Woods. By 1909, he had returned to Oak Creek and become a partner in the Mint Saloon with a Louis Schneider.[152] He purchased property and seemed to be doing well for himself until the morning of June 25, 1909. According to witnesses, Albert woke earlier than usual and went to the Mint Saloon, having the bartender open early so he could do some business. He promptly went to the back room, which they called the poker room, and locked the doors. Shortly afterward, a shot rang out, and when neighbors investigated, they found his body slumped on the floor. Albert had apparently shot himself with his .38-caliber gun through his mouth, killing himself instantly. Speculation was that it was over a quarrel he had with Miss Woods.[153]

# Chapter 13

# THE REIDYS

In July 1908, the stage arrived with W.H. Stonehouse, Hugh Conway from Cripple Creek and David J. Reidy and his wife, Belle, from Denver.[154] By the end of the month, the Reidys had established themselves as business proprietors, purchasing a tract of property downtown, including a business building from Judge Parker.[155] They expanded the business building and called it the Reidy Business Building, in which they put a grocery store and restaurant that they ran and leased out space to a barbershop. D.J. Reidy became involved in town politics, serving as a town trustee and police magistrate, and sat on a number of committees, including fire and police, franchises and ordinances. At the start, the two seemed like respectable businesspeople.

David J. Reidy, or D.J., as he was known, was born in Ireland in 1878 and immigrated to the United States in 1897 at the age of nineteen.[156] D.J. met and married Belle in Denver, Colorado, in 1906, and together they set up a business in Kremmling before heading to Oak Creek. With the Moffat Line being all the talk in the Denver papers and the towns along its path deemed prosperous investments, it seemed a natural choice for the entrepreneurial pair to relocate to the up-and-coming small town of Oak Creek. Oak Creek would provide a long-term profit for business, as there were a number of profitable mines employing numerous men.

In December 1908, D.J. Reidy applied for a saloon license and opened the Miners Exchange Saloon in his building.[157] It wasn't long after this that the Reidys lost their respectability in the community. In 1909, Reidy stopped

D.J. Reidy saloon ad. *Colorado Archives.*

Oak Creek, circa 1910. The Reidy Rooming House is the two-story structure in the lower left of the photo. Hickory Flats sat to the far right of the photo. *Tracks and Trails Museum.*

serving as a town trustee and even failed to renew his saloon license that August, but it was granted at the following town meeting in September. Mrs. Reidy established the Reidy boardinghouse in their large twelve-room house on Main Street, and it quickly became known as a house of ill repute. According to the *Oak Creek Times* on March 29, 1918, "The Reidy house was notorious throughout this portion of Colorado and women of loose reputation rode horseback through the streets, attended the picture shows, were present at public dances and held all night revelries in the big building on the corner of Main Street and Bell Avenue."[158]

In the 1910 census, two of the Reidy lodgers were even listed as prostitutes, something never seen in Northwest Colorado census records. Apparently, the census worker did not see a reason to be more discreet.[159]

In 1914, things were heating up in Oak Creek between the mine companies and the mine unions, and Reidy got himself caught up in the dispute. Reidy and Harry R. Burt, an ex–special agent for the railroad who was working in the Walker Mercantile, got into a violent altercation. Bad blood had existed between Reidy and Burt over opinions regarding the mine situation. One afternoon, Reidy loaded up on whiskey with two friends, and they came up with a plan to confront Burt while he was working. Reidy approached Burt and went to draw his gun; however, Burt was sober and quicker on the draw and shot Reidy in the throat.[160] Charges were filed once Reidy had recovered, but Burt left the area before the issue was brought to trial, so charges were dropped against Reidy.

The year 1915 proved no better for the Reidys. The Reidy house made the newspapers continuously, once over a disturbance when some of the Reidy "lady roomers" took to raising a ruckus on the streets after a night of drinking on the town, waking up town residents.[161] Then, that August, D.J. was arrested for selling whiskey in the dry district of Mount Harris. Reidy had loaded up his automobile with whiskey and some of his harem of prostitutes and proceeded to set up two large tents down by the river near the company town of Mount Harris. Mount Harris was a dry, no-liquor-allowed, company-owned coal-mining town located about twenty miles north of Oak Creek situated in the Bear Canyon near the town of Hayden.

Big Six Saloon ad. *Colorado Archives.*

Sheriff Emory Clark got word and headed to the site, where he sent in a decoy to purchase whiskey. Once he saw that it was the real stuff, he arrested Reidy and fined him $100.[162]

The town trustees finally had enough and held a special meeting in September 1915, voting unanimously to close the Reidy Resort on Main Street or else the Reidys would face legal proceedings.[163] Reidy agreed to comply with the town's ultimatum and closed his rooming house.

D.J. and Belle divorced shortly thereafter, and Belle headed up to Casper, Wyoming, changing her last name to Aldrich. She returned briefly in 1918 to see if she could reopen the resort when she heard a rumor that Oak Creek was going to be "wide open" again. She was disappointed to find out that things were not as they were rumored and ended up leaving town again, but not before she married another local cowboy.[164]

# Chapter 14

# THE RAY MURDER

Three shots rang out in the early morning hours of November 7, 1915, leaving a local saloon owner and town constable, James Ray, dead.[165] Ray had been shot by his wife of less than a year. Mary, or May, as she was also known, alleged that James had been abusing her and she shot him in self-defense.

James Ray moved to Oak Creek in 1909 and established himself as a saloon man, owning a stake in the Big Six Saloon.[166] He was well liked in the community, serving as the town constable, and had a number of friends. Mary Aline Smith had been working as a prostitute when she met and married James Ray.[167] According to the local newspapers, which may have exaggerated a bit for sensational purposes, she had been married several times before she came to Oak Creek. Regardless, she did have a ten-year-old daughter who was in a boarding school in Minnesota. Once James had married May, the little girl was sent for so that she could live with them. Later, it would come out that May had at one time trained as a nurse. Somehow, by 1908, she had made her way to Oak Creek, most likely arriving as the town started to boom.

The local newspaper had a field day with the case and depicted May in the worst possible light, running articles that told of her scandalous ways and headlines such as the one from November 15, 1915: "Kills Husband Who Takes Her from Life of Shame." Opinions were divided. Since 1900, there had been only about seven cases of women killing their husbands, and only one of those women was found guilty. Rarely was a woman convicted

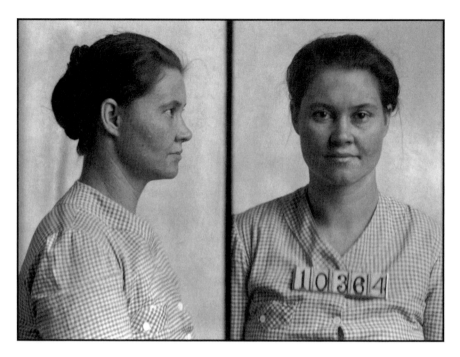

Mary or May Ray mug shot in 1916. *Colorado Archives.*

of such a crime. However, this case had a twist: the defendant's sordid past as a known prostitute.

May was arraigned and entered a plea of not guilty based on self-defense. The trial took place in January in Steamboat Springs. During the week of deliberations, events leading up to the murder came out regarding May's behavior and that of her husband. James Ray married May on March 3, 1915. Prior to her marriage, May was an inmate of the Reidy house of ill fame and had run into trouble with the law on a number of occasions while drunk. After the couple was married, May became a model housewife for about two months while they set up house and sent for her young daughter. All seemed well until that June, when she was seen with a former associate getting drunk and, according to witnesses, indulging in "her old time orgies."[168] After that, the couple was known to frequently drink and fight.

May alleged that soon after she married Ray, he started a scam of which she did not want to be part. Ray insisted on bringing home drunk men with money, or "suckers" as he called them, to their house. He would entice the men into a game of poker and then fleece them out of their money with the help of a few friends. May's objections to this ploy were allegedly the start of their estrangement. May also claimed that her husband brutally forced her to work at the lunch counter of his saloon and that he often beat her. When shown the gun, May broke down crying for the only time during the trial. She stated that she did not know where the gun had come from and that it was by sheer accident that she had come upon it while Ray was choking her, and she shot him out of self-defense.

Testimonies from locals who were friends with James Ray were very damaging to May's defense case. Stories circulated of how May had continued to frequent saloons and dances without her husband and that they had fought over her frequents visits to the house of her former employment, where she would drink while keeping company with other men. Mrs. Gustafson, a neighbor of the pair, testified that May had been drinking the day of the murder and had stopped by her house. Mrs. Gustafson stated that she had advised May to go home and get supper for her husband and that May had replied she would feed him bullets for supper; that was all the supper he would get. Another neighbor, a Mrs. John Creek, testified that May had shown her the revolver and told her that she was going to "fill her husband full of lead." Other witnesses stated that on a number of occasions, May had threatened that she would shoot her husband if he ever hit her again and that she was going to try to make him strike her. It also didn't help that May entered the courtroom smiling and showing no fear during the trial.

After a week of testimonies, the trial came to an end after eighteen hours of deliberation. The jury decided that May was guilty of murder in the second degree. Judge Shumate, who presided over the case, handed down the sentence of ten years to life in prison.

May's attorneys, A.L. Wessels and E.W. Norlin, immediately sent in an appeal to the state supreme court. May was transferred to Denver, where, during her appeals, she gave a number of interviews with the newspapers to plead her case to the public. During one of these interviews, she gave her view of her appeal case to the *Denver Post*:

> *If I obtain a new trial I am going to demand a jury of women. Strange as it may seem the men are against me and the women were for me in my trial. My husband had a lot of friends. He was a prince of a good fellow with the men and everybody liked him. He was good to me also when he was sober and I loved him more than all his friends put together but when he was under the influence of liquor he was a fiend in his home.*[169]

Although May played to the growing anti-alcohol sentiment, her case fell on deaf ears. In June 1917, the Colorado Supreme Court denied her petition without any public outcry. The court held that although the trial court in Routt County should have instructed the charge as manslaughter, the error was not enough to obtain a new trial or get a reversal of the sentence. May was moved from the Jefferson County jail to serve her sentence in the Canon City State Penitentiary.

May was paroled in October 1919 after serving just four years on her sentence.[170] May had become a model prisoner, working as a nurse and Red Cross worker. She became a skilled operator on a knitting machine, making thousands of socks for soldiers and sailors who were fighting overseas during World War I. She also was credited with tirelessly nursing patients of the influenza epidemic at coal camps near the prison. These efforts earned her recommendations for early parole from the Red Cross, as well as the warden of the prison.[171] Warden Tynan stated for the parole board that May was one of the most model prisoners he had ever known at the penitentiary; she had made a complete reformation and had become a devout Christian while at the prison.[172]

# Chapter 15

# WILLIAM DOYLE

William Doyle and his wife, Anna, arrived in Oak Creek around 1912. They quickly purchased a lot on Main Street to construct a two-story building that was to be a saloon on the main floor with a large rooming house on the second floor.[173] Doyle applied for his saloon license before the building was completed so he could open as soon as the structure was finished. However, just before the building was completed, a fire swept through Oak Creek, destroying a number of buildings, including the Doyles'. The Doyles were set back but unfazed; they started to rebuild on a new site on Sharpe Avenue and applied to the town to transfer the saloon license to the new site. This was a larger lot, and the new building would have room enough to include a hall on the back of the building for large events like dances and dinners. The application was approved, and the Doyles established their business. Things were going well for the pair for a few years until William was charged in 1915 for not adhering to the saloon closure laws, which required saloons to close at midnight. A few months later, Doyle was charged with assault and battery on a customer and was subsequently fined.

Meanwhile, the Doyles' rooming house had established a loose reputation, and eventually one of their inmates, a Laura Benton, was arrested and charged with larceny. Laura was found guilty and sentenced to the penitentiary from one to ten years for fleecing one of her customers out of thirty dollars in cash, a watch with chain and other valuables while he slept.[174]

The Doyles, like Tom Piercen, continued their business on the sly after prohibition put the saloons out of business, selling homemade booze at private backroom parties. Both husband and wife were eventually charged with bootlegging, of which they were both convicted and heavily fined.[175]

# Chapter 16
## HICKORY FLATS

Hickory Flats was a red-light section of Oak Creek located on the eastern side of town by Bell Avenue and Colfax. The residents were mostly poor or of color and lived in small shacks. A number of prostitutes made their homes there and, after prohibition, so did a number of bootleggers.

Several violent incidents and murders took place in this little neighborhood, such as the one reported in October 1916, when Emma Flores, a prostitute referred to as the Queen of Hickory Flats, drank too much one evening and decided to take a rifle and hunt down a rival of hers. She went through town causing quite a disturbance, shooting up the streets, until she was finally overpowered and arrested.[176]

After prohibition, the little neighborhood had a hard time going dry. Bootleg whiskey and private drinking establishments, as well as the number of prostitutes and amount of violence, instigated a number of police roundups of its inhabitants as a means of cleaning up this disreputable shanty-ville neighborhood.

Part V

# BEAR RIVER COLONY

Chapter 17

# HAYDEN

The area that is now Hayden was near the site established by Major J.B. Thompson and Albert Smart in 1874 as part of the Bear River Colony, which never emerged. Albert Smart's father, Porter Smart, formed the Bear River Road Company in 1873, selling stock in the company to investors.[177] He speculated that the area would boom based on the geological findings from the Ferdinand V. Hayden survey that acknowledged large coal deposits in the area, and the construction of a suitable road to travel to the remote area seemed appropriate. Interest from the Burlington Railroad seemed to solidify his belief that Northwest Colorado would be a perfect investment for speculation, and he formed the Bear River Colony with his sons, Albert and Gordon. Both Albert and Gordon homesteaded in the area, with Albert and his young family living close to Major J.B. Thompson and his family, who had a small trading post. It was implied that Thompson was selling alcohol to the Indians at his trading post, but nothing was ever reported to the authorities, and no charges were brought up against the former Indian agent. For the most part, the Thompsons and Smarts got along with the neighboring Utes on the White River Reservation, trading with them on a fairly regular basis.

When Routt County formed in 1877, Hayden was named the temporary county seat, and a cabin was constructed to house the courthouse.[178] Hayden held the position until the county held a vote in 1878 and it was decided that Hahn's Peak would become the county seat.[179] The records were moved by wagons to Hahn's Peak in the following spring of 1879.[180] It was a stroke of luck that the records were moved because that September would see the fateful Meeker incident, in the aftermath of which many of the homesteads and outbuildings in the Hayden vicinity were burned down. Most of the families who had fled the area, including the Smarts, never returned.

The next influx of people to the Hayden area was during the 1880s and included a number of families such as the Reids, the Walkers and the Fiskes. The Walkers maintained a small ranch saloon for a brief time as a gathering

Hayden in 1894. A Wallihan photo. *Hayden Heritage Center.*

George Anderson Hayden, saloon owner, in 1907. *Hayden Heritage Center.*

spot for locals and travelers; however, it was never anything more and was eventually dismantled as more people arrived to the area.

The first known business saloon was built by a man named Rube Wiley along with an associate, John X. Turner, who also ran a restaurant.[181] The Wiley saloon lasted for a few years until the owners eventually sold out and moved on. The hamlet grew larger during the 1890s, and a town site was platted. Joe Jones established a saloon on the west side of Walker Lane, now

Hayden Restaurant and Rube Wiley Saloon in Hayden in the 1890s. *Hayden Heritage Center.*

The town of Hayden. *Hayden Heritage Center.*

Walnut Street. Jones got out of the saloon business and leased the building to J.L. Norvell in June 1897. In 1906, the building was sold to George Anderson. Anderson, who hailed from Massachusetts, had opened a saloon in Hahn's Peak in 1899. As Hahn's Peak started to decline, Anderson looked for business opportunity elsewhere, finally settling on the newly incorporated town of Hayden. Hayden had an optimistic future for growth, as rumors circulated that Moffat was looking at the town as one of his main station yards. Anderson named his saloon and billiard hall the Hayden Exchange and advertised it as a "Favorite Resort for Tourists." This was the only saloon in town until Hayden's early prohibition on alcohol in 1908.[182] The saloon building was the site of the only shootout in town.

# Chapter 18

# SHOOTOUT AT JONES SALOON

In the early hours of March 1, 1897, a fury of shots rang out from the Joe Jones Saloon on Walnut Street in Hayden, leaving one man dead and another seriously injured in the street.[183] The incident grew out of a disagreement over a game of chance in the saloon between two cowboys, William Sawtelle and John Ogg, or "Texas John," as he was known.[184]

John Ogg had lost about fourteen dollars to William Sawtelle in a game of chance, either dice or poker, and felt he had been cheated. Ogg's feelings of anger grew as he continued drinking at the saloon, while Sawtelle left the saloon to attend a local dance that was being held down the street. Ogg eventually worked himself up to a fury, headed down to the dance and called Sawtelle out, demanding that he return the money he had cheated him out of. Words were exchanged as both men headed back to the saloon. Sawtelle laughingly dismissed the drunken Ogg's threats, as he didn't take him too seriously. Once they got back into the saloon, Sawtelle resumed playing cards. Ogg pulled his gun and started shooting wildly, missing his intended target. Billy McCune, who was standing by the door and had tried to run out to escape the onslaught of gunfire, was hit in the thigh. Sawtelle quickly returned fire, hitting Ogg in the chest. The two continued to trade gunfire until Ogg, in a confused state, shot McCune for the second time in the arm, thinking he was his intended target. Ogg stood in the center of the room and was noted as saying, "He hit me but I got my man." Then he promptly fell to the floor, dead.[185] Sawtelle eventually turned himself in to authorities and was acquitted by a coroner's jury that felt the shooting was an act of self-defense.[186]

Jones Saloon building, where the shootout between John Ogg and William Sawtelle took place. Later, this was Anderson's Saloon. Rumor had it that one of the bullets from the Ogg shootout remained in the wall. *Author's collection.*

Ogg was twenty-eight years old at the time of his death. He was born in Texas somewhere near San Antonio, which is how he came by the nickname of "Texas John." He supposedly killed a man while working on the D Ranch on the Red River in Indian Territory but had been acquitted of the charges, as the shooting was deemed self-defense. He was a quarter Indian and wore his hair long to remind people or intimidate them. According to the newspaper, he had a reputation for wild gunplay and getting into fights when he had drank too much alcohol. He had come to Routt County the previous August with Charles C. Wright, with whom he had a partnership in Villa Grove, Colorado, cutting ties for the railroad.[187] The previous August, he had been to Routt County to work for ex–county commissioner and surveyor Ezekiel Shelton.[188] Ogg was painted in newspapers with a reputation as being part Indian and a volatile drunk at a time of racial bigotry, so it is no wonder that Sawtelle was able to have the charges acquitted with little deliberation. The fact that Billy McCune was an innocent bystander furthered Ogg's villainy in the public eye. McCune was badly injured, requiring surgery, and it was thought he would be crippled for life. Eventually he healed; however, he was unable to return to the saddle for a number of years.

McCune was a well-liked young cowboy who worked for the Ora Haley outfit out of Laramie, Wyoming. Ora Haley was a cattle baron who employed numerous cowboys on his large cattle operation, the Two Bar Ranch, which saddled southern Wyoming and Northwest Colorado. Haley would later come to the forefront of history in the Browns Park area for hiring the notorious Tom Horn to kill alleged cattle rustlers and homestead ranchers Matt Rash and Isom Dart, who were land competitors of his. Horn, who was known for being a gun for hire in the Wyoming range wars, was eventually hanged for killing the fourteen-year-old son of a sheep rancher.

Sawtelle was vindicated in the shooting of Ogg; however, before the dust had even settled from the shooting, Sawtelle was involved in another shooting just a few weeks later in a Craig saloon that would show him in a whole different light.

Part VI
# COWBOY COUNTRY

# Chapter 19

# CRAIG

The town of Craig originally started farther east as a post office named Windsor in 1877.[189] By 1883, it had moved westward, close to its present location, where it was known as Yampah Park.[190] Located in the western part of Routt County, it was primarily an agricultural area best suited for cattle ranching and dry farming.

A number of early settlers had homesteaded in the area, including William Rose, who arrived in 1881 and homesteaded near Fortification Creek, followed by the Haugheys, Archie McLachlan, the Taylor brothers, John Mack, the Ranney brothers, the Breeze family, R.H. Green and the Teagarden family.[191] Many of the streets in Craig are named after these early settlers and community leaders. In 1887, W.H. Tucker came to the area and decided to build a town.[192] Tucker went to Denver and secured the financial backing from Frank Russell and his chief financial backer, Reverend Bayard Craig, after whom the town was named.[193]

The town grew and prospered and within a few years contained two mercantile stores, including a branch store of the Hugus Company, a blacksmith, a livery and feed barn, a saddle and harness store, a community center and the Ledford saloon.[194] The first newspaper, the *Pantagraph*, was started in 1891 by the Teagardens. Rumors had already begun circulating about the possibility of a rail line going through the area, with Burlington Line surveyors going through the area, as well as Moffat's surveyors from the Denver Northwestern looking at possibilities. The community's growth slowed down once it was realized that the rail line would be a long time in coming, if ever.

The town of Craig, circa 1910, looking southwest. *Hayden Heritage Center.*

The town of Craig looking south in 1910. The Manhattan is the tall building in the background. *Museum of Northwest Colorado.*

In 1897, a fire erupted on Valentine's Day from decorations put up in the community hall and swept through the town, destroying a number of buildings in the early business district of Yampa Avenue.[195] By 1904, the town had rebuilt its downtown area, including the construction of a second saloon, owned by Mike Smith.[196] This saloon was located where the West Theatre now sits.

Craig Saloon. *Museum of Northwest Colorado.*

In 1908, the vote went throughout the county on whether each town wanted to allow the sale of alcohol. Craig voters opted to go wet and allow the saloons to continue operating even though it had a few issues with gambling and adherence to closure hours.[197] In 1910, rumors abounded in newspapers that a proposed railroad junction would be built in Craig. The rumor proposed that the Moffat Line, which was building westward from Steamboat Springs through Craig to Salt Lake City, would connect in town with the Wamsutter-Craig Branch Line of the Union Pacific from the north, making Craig the only junction of two competing lines in Routt County.[198] This provided the area an overwhelming possibility of financial success for early investors. Craig was growing in strides when, in 1911, the large westernmost section of Routt County was divided to form Moffat County, with Craig as the county seat. Craig boasted only two saloons at that time, and it raised its saloon license fee from $500 to $700 in anticipation of a possible boom.[199] However, by 1913, the possibility of a railroad junction had become just a passing fancy. The once ambitious Moffat Railroad was broke, and the company had gone into receivership since Moffat's untimely

Craig, circa 1911. *Hayden Heritage Center.*

death. The grand dreams of the late David Moffat were fading fast, and although the line reached Craig in 1913, it would end there, never to make it to Salt Lake City as Moffat had hoped. The arrival of the train in 1913 did have positive results even without continuing to Salt Lake. It still connected the town to Denver for shipping goods to and from town, which helped the town to thrive. In addition to cattle and agriculture crops, coal became a huge export from Craig in the years to come.

For a time, the town of Craig even attracted some of the saloon men from Steamboat Springs to invest, including Shorty Anderson, who found his way to Craig and leased the Manhattan, a combination hotel, restaurant and saloon—a perfect trio for working his prostitutes. The Manhattan burned down in 1915 while Shorty was having issues with the law. Shorty had been charged with white slavery for running prostitutes at a number of his businesses, so he headed to Baggs, Wyoming, a favorite place for many who wanted to get just outside the Colorado law. The authorities finally went and forced him to return to Colorado to face the charges; however, by then prohibition had taken root. Shorty was out of business, and his girls, such as Hazel McGuire, had moved on.

Craig's main saloons were the Ledford & Kittell Saloon and the Mike Smith Saloon, both favorite spots for cowboys to go for a drink or sit for a game of cards. There is no mention of women working these two saloons, and both owners were highly respected community men.

## Chapter 20

# LEDFORD

## SALOON MAN, LAWMAN

John S. Ledford was born on May 6, 1861, in Georgia and made his way to Colorado in 1880 when he was twenty-one years old.[200] He worked as a miner, teamster and cowboy until he made his way to Routt County in 1886.[201] Ledford took up a homestead in the western portion of Routt County, now Moffat County, and drove a stage from Rawlins, Wyoming, to Meeker. In 1891, he moved to Craig and opened a livery stable, which he ran for about a year before he went into the saloon business. Ledford went in business with Kittell and ran the Ledford & Kittell Saloon, which operated under a grocer's license.[202]

In 1897, the Ledford & Kittell Saloon was the scene of a shooting involving William "Billy" Sawtelle, who just a few months earlier in nearby Hayden had shot and killed John Ogg in the Joe Jones Saloon. The shooting in Craig happened in the early morning of April 15, 1897.[203] Sawtelle had been drinking and playing poker all night with a young man named Kent Whiting in the front room of the saloon. Whiting, who was originally from New York and had recently returned from a stint in the Spanish-American War in Cuba, was in town visiting a local rancher for the summer.[204] In the early hours of the morning, the two were about to break from their game when Sawtelle jumped up and shot Whiting. According to Whiting, they had been on good terms all evening when all of a sudden Sawtelle, who had won the last hand, jumped up and started waving his gun at him. Whiting was unarmed at the time and just threw up his arms, begging for Sawtelle not to shoot him. Whiting fortunately darted to the side just as Sawtelle shot at him,

Ledford Saloon in Craig. *Museum of Northwest Colorado.*

and the bullet hit him in the shoulder rather than the chest. Before Sawtelle could get another shot at him, Whiting ran into the back room, where the owner, John Ledford, was sleeping. Ledford was able to calm Sawtelle down and convince him to drop his gun. Ledford then proceeded to call on the local doctor to attend to Whiting's wound. Meanwhile, Sawtelle hopped onto his horse and rode out of town, leaving fifty dollars at the saloon to pay for Whiting's medical treatment.[205]

By November of that same year, it would come out that Sawtelle was a member of a gang of highwaymen and cattle thieves in Northwest Colorado.[206] Sawtelle was later rumored also to have been in the employ of Ora Haley, a rancher who was known to hire gunmen of ill repute such as the likes of Tom Horn to remove impediments to his large cattle operation. Sawtelle gained a reputation as a gunman and would be involved in a number of "self-defense" and "accidental" shootings in Northwest Colorado and in the vicinity of Laramie, Wyoming, over the next several years, killing at least one man in Wyoming.[207] Things finally got too sticky for him with the law, and he left for South America in 1910, spending four years there.[208] In 1914, he returned to the United States, visiting Wyoming before heading to Nevada, where he was eventually killed in a saloon shootout in February 1916, dying as he had lived—with a gun in his hand.[209]

John Ledford served as a game warden and had a successful ranch outside town. He was appointed sheriff of the newly formed Moffat

County after its division from Routt County in 1911. By 1914, Ledford's saloon, known as the Korner Grocery, was destroyed by fire one night when the stove in the restaurant in the adjacent building was left open, destroying both businesses. All that remained of the saloon and restaurant was a large hole. Ledford left the saloon business for good and focused on his ranching interests and law enforcement.

In 1916, excavation was started on the site for the First National Bank building, which was being constructed on the site of the Korner Grocery. While the workers were digging, they struck glass. Upon closer scrutiny, they discovered the glass was quart-size bottles containing beer kept cold in the soft earth. Much to the workers' surprise and delight, the fire in 1914 had not consumed all the liquor that had been stored in the saloon's basement. The workers continued to unearth a large supply of beers that, to their pleasure, were ice cold. The laborers were aware that it was illegal to offer one another a drink and instead used sign language to disperse the uninjured bottles to one another. It seems they were very cautious with the rest of the excavation, even spending extra time digging the hole far deeper than needed just in case any more bottles could be found.[210]

# Chapter 21

# MIKE SMITH

Mike Smith was another pioneer character who must have seen the golden opportunity of future development of the area and hung up his spurs to go into the saloon business. He built Craig's second saloon, the Club Saloon, generally referred to as Mike Smith's saloon.

Mike was born on August 26, 1855, in Ireland and received his education in London before arriving in America as a young man in 1873. He headed westward, living for a time in Quincy, Illinois, and then moving on to Fremont County. He moved about, even working for the railroad for a time before arriving in Routt County in 1882. By this time, Mike had met and married his wife, Mary, in 1878 and had two young daughters when he homesteaded a ranch near the lower Elkhead, about six miles east of the present site of the city of Craig and close to the present-day county line division between Routt and Moffat County.

Mike worked as a cowboy and built up his ranch for a number of years while his family expanded to include six daughters. As the town of Craig developed and rumors abounded regarding the coming of the railroad, Mike seized the opportunity and invested his money by purchasing a number of town lots. In 1904, he built the town's second saloon on the site now occupied by the West Theatre.

Politics were very important to Mike, who was a lifelong Democrat. Mike hired Will Kitchens in 1906 to be his "chief engineer" at his "wet goods emporium," which gave Mike more time to pursue his political interests. This enabled him to attend the Democratic State Convention in 1906 as a representative for Routt County along with C.H. Leckenby, J.H. Crawford, B.L. Jefferson, A.M. Gooding, R.E. Norvell and Willard Peck.

Things were pretty quiet and financially going well for the Smiths. In 1909, Mike decided to retire from ranching and leased his ranch out to Henry Etzler. Mike purchased a house in Denver on Acoma Street, where Mary and the five youngest girls moved for better educational advantages for the girls. Mike would divide his time in Denver and Craig watching over his ranching investments, business interests and the saloon.

Gruff on the exterior, Mike supposedly had a soft, charitable spot for others who were struggling. Supposedly, he didn't like people to see this side of him; only his closest associates knew of how he helped sign notes for failing businesses, anonymously paid doctor's bills and hospital bills for struggling families and helped save a few families from being foreclosed on their mortgages.

When prohibition came to the state in 1916, Mike closed down his saloon. He stayed on in Craig, managing his various businesses, and decided to run for the state legislature as the Democratic candidate. It wasn't long after he issued his intentions and received the majority of votes designating him as a candidate for the state legislature that he was thrown into the hotbed of a sensational political plot. That March, Mike was accused and charged with bootlegging for selling a bottle of whiskey to a man by the name of Baker. By August, it would come out that the entire charge was a political ploy to bring about Smith's downfall in the ensuing election. The main witness was a man who had owed Smith money for over two years and was supposedly pushed into testifying against Smith by another politician. Mike was acquitted and, unnerved, still ran for the state legislature, although he did not win.

Mike was not without getting in trouble. In 1915, he was arrested in Steamboat's Brooklyn district along with Gus Durbin and a number of Brooklyn inmates.[211] He was quickly released, but it was not his last run-in with the law.

After prohibition in Colorado, in 1917 Mike ran into considerable trouble with the authorities concerning the illegal possession of whiskey. One evening, Mike accompanied two other men to Baggs, Wyoming. Once they got to Baggs, one of the men, who was from Oak Creek, was arrested for charges stemming from a district court case regarding improper behavior with a young woman. Apparently, this was his second time charged with such an act; the first time, the young man married the young lady in question and later secured an annulment. This time he was not as fortunate and faced criminal charges. This did not deter Mike or the driver, Tom Cassidy, from their plans of imbibing a few drinks since prohibition laws had not yet taken hold in Wyoming. The two men supposedly purchased and consumed a large amount of whiskey before heading back to Craig. Sheriff Clark got wind of the two men's purchases and intention of bringing whiskey into the now dry state of Colorado. The sheriff decided to catch the two men on their drive back to Craig, so he lay in wait on the road west of Hayden. The sheriff stopped the pair, who were inebriated, and searched the vehicle, where he found a suitcase with five full quarts of whiskey and one partially empty bottle that the two had drunk on their drive back.[212] According to one story, Mike denied drinking in Colorado and said that they had swigged a large amount on the other side of the state line just before leaving for the long drive home. Another version was that Mike told the sheriff that the liquor was old stock that he just happened to have on him. Either way, they were both arrested and charged with bootlegging, as well as moving liquor, which was a serious charge. The charges were later dropped against the two when the paperwork was shown to have been filed incorrectly.[213] Smith's ability to evade having negative articles written about him in Craig's local newspaper, the *Empire*, was attributed by the *Routt County Sentinel* editor to his political connections with the *Empire* newspaper as one of its largest backers and thus "string puller."[214]

In June 1919, Mike was doing another trip to Baggs with a couple friends when he accidentally fell out of the automobile on the return trip. Mike had been sitting in the backseat when the car apparently hit a very large pothole, which pitched the vehicle about so violently that it ejected him. The driver and front passenger did not realize that Mike had been thrown from the vehicle until they arrived in Craig. A search party was put together, and Mike was found near the road unconscious with a broken collarbone and miscellaneous scrapes and bruises, the most serious on his head. Things looked grim for the old saloonkeeper, and many believed that he would not survive his injuries. Mike's family took him to a Denver hospital, where he recuperated for a few months and was well enough within a year to visit Craig to check on his business concerns with one of his daughters. Mike gave every appearance of making a full recovery until the summer of 1924, when he told his family he had not long to live. He passed away shortly thereafter in August of the same year.

# Part VII
# DRY TIMES

# Chapter 22

# THE TEMPERANCE MOVEMENT AND THE END OF AN ERA

The temperance movement to eradicate society's evils by eliminating alcohol availability gained momentum, especially with women, toward the end of the nineteenth century and the beginning of the twentieth century. As more families moved westward toward the later part of the nineteenth century, a clash of moral integrity occurred, and the saloons and brothels that had openly plied their wares and trade on the early frontier came under scrutiny. At first, church and moral purity groups pushed to segregate the saloons and brothels from the respectable parts of town, creating saloon districts and red-light districts that gave the dominant male western element an outlet for its socially depraved behavior. This attitude was best summed up by an 1892 newspaper editorial:

> *Like gambling, it* [prostitution] *is ineradicable, yet—if handled properly, it can be curtailed. Against houses of ill fame, the Mascot makes no crusade, so long as they are not located in respectable neighborhoods, for they are a necessary evil. The subject is a delicate one to handle, but it must be admitted that such places are necessary in ministering to the passions of men who otherwise would be tempted to seduce young ladies of their acquaintance.*[215]

Although accepted by some, many individuals felt that alcohol, prostitution and gambling were the leading causes of social ills that plagued society and threatened decency and family values. A number of organized groups formed in order to right some of the social ills of the period brought on by the "loosening of morals" after the Civil War and subsequent western expansion. These groups focused their moral purity attacks to eradicate forms of vice such as drinking, gambling, pornography, white slavery and prostitution. One of the strongest groups to attack vice was the Woman's Christian Temperance Union, which later became the General Federation of Women's Clubs. These groups advocated for new laws against vice and were able to push saloons and prostitution almost completely underground.[216] These women's groups later spearheaded the prohibition movement across the country, including in Colorado.

In 1909 in Denver, Colorado, the Supreme Court upheld an earlier ruling that allowed for dry wards to oust over "nine saloons and 3 drug stores" from their districts.[217] Criticism ran strong in Steamboat for the dual policy of not allowing alcohol in the town proper yet allowing alcohol and vice just a stone's throw across the river. In 1902, Mrs. James Crawford led the Woman's Christian Union in Steamboat Springs. The group's main objections at first were against the temperance saloons and billiard halls on the town side that allowed young boys to gamble. Later, it pushed for the tenets of the temperance movement and pressured local politicians to do something about the issue of illegal gambling and illicit behavior in rowdy Brooklyn. In 1912, Steamboat Springs adopted the "Criminal Code" that pressured the local sheriff to crack down on violations that included "offenses against persons property, against the public peace, justice, morality, health, forgery, offenses by cheats, swindlers, confidence games, fakers, prize fights, false weights, measures and the like, prostitutes, and the keeping of houses of prostitution, gambling in all its forms, pool halls, and permitting minors therein, bootlegging and violations of the anti-saloon laws."[218]

The temperance movement played an important role in the political tug of war between the Republican and Democratic Parties across the country, including in Routt County. The Republican candidates took on the temperance cause as a political reform platform while trying to make the Democrats look like pro-vice villains. Most saloon owners were Democrats, as were a majority of Catholics and immigrants, creating a large political force. The Republican Party used these factors to influence votes from the more liberal Republicans, conservative Democrats and politically nonaffiliated. Local politics conveyed some of this posturing in the April 2, 1915 *Routt County Sentinel* article entitled "Good Citizenship Republican Slogan," which posed this question:

> *If the candidates for town offices on the Democratic ticket stand for the strict enforcement of law and the ordinances, why is it that every saloon*

*keeper, every inmate of the houses of ill-fame, and every gambler in the corporate limits of Steamboat Springs, is working night and day against the Republican ticket? Is it possible that Brooklyn can control the destinies of Steamboat Springs?*

The final blow for the saloon crowd came on January 1, 1916, when Colorado passed a law prohibiting alcohol, making the entire state dry. This ended the open era for the red-light districts in Colorado. Saloons shut down across the state, and saloon owners either adapted or moved on. This did not fully curtail the drinking and vice, as many thought it would, as bootlegging, private drinking parties and prostitution would still occur; they were just less out in the open. The newspapers were filled with stories of bootleggers being fined and loose women, former inmates of well-known establishments, still conducting business. Instances of violence and tragedy still occurred, such as the three young men in Hayden who had an odd notion to get drunk by drinking hair tonic, erroneously thinking that wood alcohol was the same as drinking alcohol, and died. Eventually, the notoriety of these red-light districts would become the stuff of legends, and its inhabitants slipped into the obscurity of time.

# NOTES

## CHAPTER 1

1. *Steamboat Pilot*, "Steamboat Springs Past, Present and Future," 3–4.
2. *Silver Cliff Rustler*, "Moffat Road Financed."
3. *Aspen Daily Times*, "Through Line Soon."

## CHAPTER 2

4. Stanko, Towler and Seligson, *Historical Guide to Routt County*, 65.
5. Stukey, "Scholars Write of Steamboat."
6. *Steamboat Pilot*, "Steamboat Springs Past, Present, and Future," 3–4.
7. Ibid.
8. Ibid.
9. Leslie, *Anthracite, Barbee, and Tosh*, 91.
10. Ibid., 92.
11. Burroughs, *Where the West Stayed Young*, 296.
12. Burroughs, *Steamboat in the Rockies*.
13. Burroughs, *Where the West Stayed Young*, 296.

## CHAPTER 3

14. *Routt County Sentinel*, June 26, 1903.
15. Ibid.
16. Burroughs, *Steamboat in the Rockies*.
17. Burroughs, *Where the West Stayed Young*, 296.
18. *Steamboat Pilot*, "Tales of Early Days."

19. Hoar, "They Would Serve You Beer," 13.
20. Ibid., 12.
21. *Routt County Sentinel*, "Jungle News," 1.
22. Burroughs, *Where the West Stayed Young*, 296.
23. *Steamboat Pilot*, "New Liquor Ordinance," 2.
24. Ibid.

# CHAPTER 4

25. *Routt County Sentinel*, "Ordinance," 2.
26. *Routt County Sentinel*, "Pin Ears Mastered in Denver Exhibition," 1.
27. *Routt County Republican*, "Bear River Valley League," 1.
28. *Routt County Sentinel*, "Big Contest," 1.
29. *Elbert County Banner*, July 8, 1904, 4.
30. *Routt County Sentinel*, "Country Press on the Ball Game," 1.
31. *Steamboat Pilot*, "History and Members of the Pioneer Association," 3.
32. "Boxing," en.wikipedia.org/wiki/boxing (accessed August 12, 2013).

# CHAPTER 5

33. *Routt County Sentinel*, "Rev. Mr. Evans Was in Court," 1.
34. *Routt County Sentinel*, "Deacon Sells," 1.
35. "United States Census, 1900," Flagstaff City, Coconino, Arizona Territory, United States.
36. Frentress (Durbin) family notes.
37. "United States Census, 1900," Flagstaff City, Coconino, Arizona Territory, United States.
38. Ibid.
39. *Arizona Champion–Coconino Sun*, 7.
40. Frentress (Durbin) family notes.
41. *Routt County Sentinel*, "Pure Local Notes," 1.
42. Hoar, "They Would Serve You Beer," 15.
43. *Routt County Sentinel*, "Deacon Sells," 1.
44. "United States Census, 1910," Precinct 21, Routt, Colorado.
45. *Routt County Sentinel*, "Local and Personal Doings," 4.
46. *Steamboat Pilot*, August 15, 1906, 4.
47. "United States Census, 1910," Precinct 21, Routt, Colorado.
48. *Routt County Sentinel*, "Jungle News," 1.
49. *Steamboat Pilot*, "Visited Brooklyn," 1.
50. Ibid.
51. *Steamboat Pilot*, "Committees Named," 3.
52. *Routt County Sentinel*, "Splendid New Ticket," 1.
53. *Routt County Sentinel*, "Eagles Organize and Have Big Spread," 1.
54. *Routt County Sentinel*, "Brooklyn Boys Show Steamboat," 1.

55. *Routt County Sentinel*, "Brief Session District Court," 1.

56. Wren, "Shady Side of the River," 30–31.

57. *Routt County Sentinel*, "Local News of the Week," 5.

58. "United States Census, 1940," Augustine, Corona, Temescal Judicial Township, Riverside, California, United States.

59. "California Death Index, 1940–1997," Augustine Durbin, 1942.

60. *Routt County Sentinel*, "Old Landmark Disappears," 1.

61. *Routt County Sentinel*, "Brooklyn Coming to the Front," 1.

62. *Steamboat Pilot*, "Steamboat Celebration Will Be Biggest Ever," 1.

63. *Routt County Sentinel*, August 7, 1914, 4.

64. *Routt County Sentinel*, "Much Property Lost in Two Bad Fires," 1.

65. *Routt County Sentinel*, "Fire Destroys Big Craig Hotel," 1.

66. *Steamboat Pilot*, "Shorty Anderson Dead at Pershing," 4.

67. "United States Census, 1900," Hayden, Routt County, Colorado, United States.

68. Ibid.

69. *Steamboat Pilot*, May 2, 1906, 4.

70. *Routt County Sentinel*, "Knocks and Boosts," 1.

71. *Steamboat Pilot*, "Boxing Contest," 1.

72. "Boxing," en.wikipedia.org/wiki/boxing (accessed August 12, 2013).

73. *Steamboat Pilot*, "McAlpine-Williams Mill Was a Hot One," 1.

# CHAPTER 6

74. Lodge, *Investigation Relative to Wages*, 1244.

75. Rutter, *Upstairs Girls*, 7.

76. Ibid.

77. Ibid.

78. U.S. Census, 1910.

79. *Steamboat Pilot*, "County Records," 1.

80. *Herald Democrat*, "Ollie Patterson's Body," 2.

81. *Routt County Sentinel*, "Considerable Smoke," 1.

82. U.S. Census, Routt County, 1910.

83. Merrill, *Steamboat Springs*, 15.

84. Spooner, "Mt. Harris," 7.

85. U.S. Census, Routt County, 1910.

86. Wren, "Shady Side of the River," 30–31.

87. U.S. Census, Routt County, 1910.

88. Ibid.

89. *Routt County Sentinel*, "Attempts to Go Suicide Route," 1.

90. *Routt County Sentinel*, "Realty Transfers," 3.

91. *Routt County Sentinel*, "Alleged Dynamiters Arrested," 8.

92. *Routt County Sentinel*, "Poor Shot," 4.

93. State of Wyoming, Bureau of Vital Statistics, Death Certificate, Evanston, WY State Hospital for the Insane, 1914, no. 987.

94. *Routt County Sentinel*, "Brooklyn Wedding."
95. *Steamboat Pilot*, December 24, 1913.

# CHAPTER 7

96. *Routt National Forest History*.
97. Ibid.
98. Wren, "Shady Side of the River," 30–31.
99. *Routt County Sentinel*, "Shooting Affray," 1.
100. Ibid.
101. *Steamboat Pilot*, "'Tex' Williams Is Dead," 1.
102. *Routt County Sentinel*, "Discovery," 1.

# CHAPTER 8

103. Stanko, Towler and Seligson, *Historical Guide to Routt County*, 77.
104. Ibid.
105. Ibid.
106. Leslie, *Anthracite, Barbee, and Tosh*, 72.
107. Ibid., 71.
108. *Yampa Leader*, June 13, 1903, 5.
109. Ibid.
110. *Yampa Leader*, "Legal Notices," 5.
111. *Yampa Leader*, "Special Town Meeting," 4.
112. *Yampa Leader*, "Local News," January 1, 1909, 8.
113. *Yampa Leader*, "Local News," May 14, 1909, 8.
114. *Yampa Leader*, "Local News'" February 5, 1909, 8.
115. *Yampa Leader*, "License Hiked to $1,000," 1.
116. Ore, "Yampa," 7.
117. *Yampa Leader*, "Royal Changes Hands," 1.
118. Stanko, Towler and Seligson, *Historical Guide to Routt County*, 80.

# CHAPTER 9

119. *Steamboat Pilot*, "Tales of the Early Days," 3.
120. United States Census, Colorado, 1880.
121. *Leadville Daily Herald*, "Joe Ward's Second Man," 4.
122. Ibid.
123. Colorado Archives, Colorado Penitentiary Records, Joseph Ward.
124. *Leadville Daily Herald*, "Joe Ward's Second Man," 4.
125. *Steamboat Pilot*, "Tales of the Early Days," 5.
126. *Steamboat Pilot*, "Tales of the Old West," 7.
127. *Cheyenne Daily Sun*, "Bear River Tragedy," 3.

128. Ibid.
129. *Steamboat Pilot*, "Tales of the Early Days," 5.
130. Ibid.
131. Ibid.

# CHAPTER 10

132. Stanko, Towler and Seligson, *Historical Guide to Routt County*, 57.
133. Ibid.
134. Leslie, *Anthracite, Barbee, and Tosh*, 98.
135. Ibid.
136. *Yampa Leader*, "Huggins Now a City," 1.
137. *Yampa Leader*, "Huggins Is Enjoined," 1.
138. Stanko, Towler and Seligson, *Historical Guide to Routt County*, 57.
139. *Oak Creek Times*, "Ordinance No. 33," 8.

# CHAPTER 11

140. United States Census, Colorado, 1910.
141. *Steamboat Pilot*, "Thomas Piercen," 1.
142. *Oak Creek Times*, "Tom Piercen Bound Over," 1.
143. *Yampa Leader*, March 18, 1910, 8.
144. *Routt County Sentinel*, "Slashed Almost Into Ribbons," 1.
145. *Steamboat Pilot*, "Mrs. Louisa Piercen," 7.
146. *Steamboat Pilot*, "District Court Will Open Here Monday April 3," 1.
147. Yurich, *Oak Creek, Colorado*.

# CHAPTER 12

148. *Oak Creek Times*, "Albert Severson Commits Suicide," 1.
149. *Oak Creek Times*, "Town Officials Confident," 1.
150. Ibid.
151. *Oak Creek Times*, "Local News," September 3, 1908, 4.
152. Ibid., May 20, 1909, 8.
153. *Oak Creek Times*, "Albert Severson Commits Suicide," 1.

# CHAPTER 13

154. *Oak Creek Times*, "Local News," July 16, 1908, 4.
155. *Oak Creek Times*, "Judge Parker Sells His Property," 1.
156. United States Census, Routt County, Colorado, 1910.
157. *Oak Creek Times*, "Local News," December 10, 1908, 4.
158. *Oak Creek Times*, "Plan to Open Up Old Reidy Resort," 1.

159. United States Census, Oak Creek, Routt County, 1910.
160. *Steamboat Pilot*, "Many Charges Grow Out of Oak Creek Shooting," 1.
161. *Oak Creek Times*, "Nice Affair," 1.
162. *Oak Creek Times*, "Dave Reidy Pays," 1.
163. *Oak Creek Times*, "Town Trustees Hold Important Meeting," 1.
164. *Routt County Sentinel*, "Among Our Neighbors," 4.

# CHAPTER 14

165. *Steamboat Pilot*, "James Ray Killed," 1.
166. *Oak Creek Times*, "Kills Husband," 1.
167. Ibid.
168. *Steamboat Pilot*, "Murder in the Second Degree," 1.
169. *Oak Creek Times*, "Mrs. Ray Says She Will Demand Jury Composed of Women," 1.
170. *Oak Creek Times*, "Mrs. Mary Ray to Be Paroled," 1.
171. *Steamboat Pilot*, "May Ray Won Her Freedom," 5.
172. Ibid.

# CHAPTER 15

173. *Steamboat Pilot*, "Watch Oak Creek Grow," 1.
174. *Oak Creek Times*, "Laura Benton Found Guilty," 1.
175. *Oak Creek Times*, "Mr. & Mrs. Doyle Given Heavy Fines," 1.

# CHAPTER 16

176. *Oak Creek Times*, "Queen of Hickory Flats," 1.

# CHAPTER 17

177. Museum of Northwest Colorado. Stock Certificate, Bear River Road, Porter Smart.
178. *Steamboat Pilot*, "Officers Who Guided Routt County," 5.
179. Ibid.
180. Ibid.
181. Leslie, Compilations of Town Businesses.
182. Ibid.

# CHAPTER 18

183. *Steamboat Pilot*, "Recalls a Tragedy," 2.
184. *Aspen Daily Times*, "Shooting at Hayden," March 2, 1897, 1.

185. Ibid.
186. Ibid.
187. "Homicide at Hayden," transcribed newspaper from Ancestry.com under "William Sawtelle," March 13, 1897.
188. Ibid.

# CHAPTER 19

189. Leslie, *Anthracite, Barbee, and Tosh*, 206.
190. Ibid., 71.
191. Craig-Moffat Golden Jubilee Committee, "First Twenty Years in Craig," 29.
192. Ibid.
193. Ibid.
194. *Steamboat Pilot*, "Craig and Its Splendid Resources," 4.
195. Ibid.
196. Ibid., 30.
197. *Oak Creek Times*, "Several Precincts in Routt County," 1.
198. *Steamboat Pilot*, "County News," 1.
199. *Oak Creek Times*, "Several Precincts in Routt County," 1.

# CHAPTER 20

200. *Craig Empire Courier*, "John S. Ledford."
201. Ibid.
202. *Steamboat Pilot*, "County Commissioners," 1.
203. *Herald Democrat*, "Around the State," 4.
204. "Sawtell Suddenly Skips," *Empire Courier*, transcribed newspaper article, April 17, 1897.
205. Ibid.
206. *Idaho Statesman*, "Organized Highwaymen."
207. *Wind River Mountaineer*, "Former Wyoming Man Killed," 1.
208. *Carbon County Journal*, October 9, 1914, 5.
209. *Rawlins Republican*, "Old Time Gambler Killed," 5.
210. *Steamboat Pilot*, "Town Goes Wet."

# CHAPTER 21

211. *Routt County Republican*, "Chiv Rounds Them Up," 1.
212. *Routt County Sentinel*, "In Jail after Baggs Auto Trip," 1.
213. *Routt County Republican*, "Court News," 1.
214. *Routt County Republican*, "Empire Editor Brays," 4.

# CHAPTER 22

215. Rosen, *Lost Sisterhood*, 5.
216. Rutter, *Upstairs Girls*, 104.
217. *Steamboat Pilot*, October 13, 1909.
218. *Routt County Sentinel*, "Grand Jury Starts General Clean Up of Bootlegging and Gambling," 1.

# BIBLIOGRAPHY

*Arizona Champion–Coconino Sun*, April 26, 1894.

*Aspen Daily Times*. "Shooting at Hayden." March 2, 1897.

———. "A Through Line Soon." March 22 1902. www.coloradohistoricnewspapers. org. Accessed September 1, 2013.

Athearn, F.J. *An Isolated Empire: History of Northwest Colorado*. 3rd ed. CO: Colorado State Office Bureau of Land Management, 1981.

Burroughs, J.R. *Steamboat in the Rockies*. Fort Collins, CO: Old Army Press, 1974.

———. *Where the West Stayed Young*. New York: William Morrow, 1962.

*Carbon County Journal*, October 9, 1914.

*Cheyenne Daily Sun*. "Bear River Tragedy." July 7, 1885. www.coloradohistoricnewspapers. org. Accessed May 14, 2013.

*Craig Empire Courier*. "John S. Ledford, Early Settler, Dies in Denver." May 12, 1937.

Craig-Moffat Golden Jubilee Committee. "The First Twenty Years in Craig." In *Craig-Moffat Golden Jubilee: Fifty Years of Progress, 1908–1958*. Craig, CO, 1958.

Dodder, J. "Brooklyn Was Bawdy, Brazen, and Bustling." *Steamboat Pilot*, December 22, 1988.

*Elbert County Banner*, July 8, 1904.

*Empire Courier*. "John S. Ledford, Early Settler, Dies in Denver." May 12, 1937.

*Herald Democrat*. "Around the State." April 22, 1897.

———. "Ollie Patterson's Body." July 27, 1892.

Hine, R.V., and J.M. Faragher. *The American West: A New Interpretive History*. New Haven, CT: Yale University Press, 2000.

Hoar, N. "They Would Serve You Beer, Whiskey, Anything You Wanted, Even Not Nice Girls." *Three Wire Winter*, 1982.

*Idaho Statesman*. "Organized Highwaymen Terrorize Northwestern Colorado." November 18, 1897.

Kelley, C. *The Outlaw Trail: The Story of Butch Cassidy and the Wild Bunch*. New York: Bonanza Books, 1959.

*Leadville Daily Herald.* "Joe Wards Second Man." October 29, 1884.

Leslie, Jan. *Anthracite, Barbee, and Tosh: The History of Routt County and Its Post Offices, 1875–1971.* Hayden, CO: Walnut Street Publishers, 2005.

———. Compilations of Town Businesses, Hayden Heritage Center Leslie Collection, unpublished.

Lodge, Henry Cabot. *Investigation Relative to Wages and Prices of Commodities.* Vol. 3. Washington, D.C.: Government Printing Office, 1911.

Marsh, C.S. *People of the Shining Mountains.* Boulder, CO: Pruett Pub. Co., 1982.

Merrill, M.S. *Steamboat Springs: Memories of a Young Colorado Pioneer.* Lake City, CO: Western Reflections Pub. Co., 2008.

Montgomery, C.L. "The History of Routt County, CO." Master's thesis, Colorado State College of Education, 1938.

*Oak Creek Times.* "Albert Severson Commits Suicide." July 1, 1909. www.coloradohistoricnewspapers.org. Accessed April 8, 2013.

———. "Big Docket for Routt." December 30, 1915. www.coloradohistoricnewspapers.org. Accessed March 8, 2013.

———. "Dave Reidy Pays One Hundred Dollar Fine." August 26, 1915. www.coloradohistoricnewspapers.org. Accessed April 10, 2013.

———. "Extra! Extra! Incendiary Fire Causes $20,000 Loss." October 31, 1912. www.coloradohistoricnewspapers.org. Accessed July 24, 2013.

———. "Fire Destroys Reidy Home." November 30, 1911. www.coloradohistoricnewspapers.org. Accessed April 8, 2013

———. "Jack Mann Found Guilty." June 8, 1911. www.coloradohistoricnewspapers.org. Accessed February 4, 2013.

———. "Judge Parker Sells His Property to New Arrivals." July 23, 1908. www.coloradohistoricnewspapers.org. Accessed July 26, 2013.

———. "Jury Holds Wife Guilty." January 21, 1916. www.coloradohistoricnewspapers.org. Accessed April 8, 2013.

———. "Kills Husband Who Takes Her from Life of Shame." November 11, 1915. www.coloradohistoricnewspapers.org. Accessed April 8, 2013.

———. "Laura Benton Found Guilty." January 26, 1917. www.coloradohistoricnewspapers.org. Accessed April 8, 2013.

———. "Local News." December 10, 1908. www.coloradohistoricnewspapers.org. Accessed July 26, 2013.

———. "Local News." July 16, 1908. www.coloradohistoricnewspapers.org. Accessed July 26, 2013.

———. "Local News." May 20, 1909.

———. "Local News." September 3, 1908.

———. "Mr. & Mrs. Doyle Given Heavy Fines." March 30, 1916.

———. "Mrs. Mary Ray Must Serve Her Sentence." June 8, 1917. www.coloradohistoricnewspapers.org. Accessed May 14, 2013.

———. "Mrs. Mary Ray to Be Paroled." October 3, 1919.

———. "Mrs. Ray Says She Will Demand Jury Composed of Women." February 24, 1916.

———. "New Officers of Town Meet." May 6, 1909. www.coloradohistoricnewspapers.org. Accessed July 24, 2013.

———. "Nice Affair." May 27, 1915. www.coloradohistoricnewspapers.org. Accessed April 8, 2013.

———. "Ordinance No. 33." July 7, 1910.

———. "Plan to Open Up Old Reidy Resort." March 29, 1918. www.coloradohistoricnewspapers.org. Accessed April 15, 2013.

———. "Queen of Hickory Flats Hunts Rival with Gun." October 5, 1916. www.coloradohistoricnewspapers.org. Accessed January 15, 2013.

———. "Real Estate Transfers." July 30, 1908. www.coloradohistoricnewspapers.org. Accessed July 9, 2013.

———. "Several Precincts in Routt County Become Anti Saloon." November 12, 1908.

———. "Sheriff Clark Takes Mrs. Mary Ray to Pen." November 2, 1917. www.coloradohistoricnewspapers.org. Accessed April 8, 2013.

———. "Tom Piercen Bound Over." November 17, 1910. www.coloradohistoricnewspapers.org. Accessed March 8, 2013.

———. "Tom Piercen Has Narrow Escape." February 9, 1911. www.coloradohistoricnewspapers.org. Accessed July 27, 2013.

———. "Town Board Meeting." August 22, 1912. www.coloradohistoricnewspapers.org. Accessed July 24, 2013.

———. "Town Board Meeting." December 9, 1909. www.coloradohistoricnewspapers.org. Accessed July 26, 2013.

———. "Town Officials Confident Injunction Only Temporary." August 13, 1908. www.coloradohistoricnewspapers.org. Accessed July 26, 2013.

———. "Town Trustees Hold Important Meeting." September 9, 1915.

———. "Watch Oak Creek." December 12, 1912. www.coloradohistoricnewspapers.org. Accessed July 24, 2013.

———. "Watch Oak Creek Grow." August 8, 1912. www.coloradohistoricnewspapers.org. Accessed July 24, 2013.

———. "Wholesale Indictment of Oak Creek Law Breakers." January 19, 1917.

Olsen, D. *Steamboat Springs Legends: A Centennial Collection.* Virginia Beach, VA: Donning Co. Pub., 1999.

Ore, Mrs. Fred. "Yampa." *Steamboat Pilot*, October 7, 1937.

*Rawlins Republican.* "Old Time Gambler Killed." February 3, 1916.

Records of Convicts. Colorado State Penitentiary. May Ray, 1917. Colorado State Archives.

Rosen, Ruth. *The Lost Sisterhood: Prostitution in America, 1900–1918.* Baltimore, MD: Johns Hopkins University Press, 1982.

*Routt County Republican.* "Alleged Dynamiters Arrested." August 4, 1911. www.coloradohistoricnewspapers.org. Accessed February 26, 2009.

———. "Bear River Valley League." May 15, 1914.

———. "Brooklyn Going Dry." November 27, 1914. www.coloradohistoricnewspapers.org. Accessed November 7, 2009.

———. "Chiv Rounds Them Up." September 17, 1915.

———. "City Rounds Them Up." September 17, 1915. www.coloradohistoricnewspapers.org. Accessed September 25, 2009.

———. "Court News." July 27, 1917.

———. "Court Work." October 9, 1914. www.coloradohistoricnewspapers.org. Accessed November 7, 2009.

———. "Empire Editor Brays." March 24, 1916.

———. July 16, 1915. www.coloradohistoricnewspapers.org. Accessed October 25, 2009.

*Routt County Sentinel.* "Alleged Dynamiters Arrested." August 4, 1911.

———. "Among Our Neighbors," April 5, 1918.

———. "Another Session of District Court." August 21, 1903. www.coloradohistoricnewspapers.org. Accessed February 17, 2009.

———. "Attempts to Go Suicide Route." November 12, 1909. www.coloradohistoricnewspapers.org. Accessed February 14, 2009.

———. August 21, 1914. www.coloradohistoricnewspapers.org. Accessed February 18, 2009.

———. "Baseball League Organized." May 15, 1914. www.coloradohistoricnewspapers.org. Accessed November 8, 2009.

———. "The Big Contest." July 1, 1904.

———. "Brief Session District Court." August 14, 1914.

———. "Brooklyn Boys Show Steamboat How to Handle Water." July 14, 1911.

———. "Brooklyn Coming to the Front." June 18, 1908. www.coloradohistoricnewspapers.org. Accessed February 15, 2009.

———. "A Brooklyn Wedding." March 4, 1910. www.coloradohistoricnewspapers.org. Accessed February 11, 2010.

———. "Considerable Smoke." December 24, 1909. www.coloradohistoricnewspapers.org. Accessed October 4, 2013.

———. "The Country Press on the Ball Game." July 15, 1904.

———. "The Deacon Sells." March 1, 1912.

———. "Discovery." March 22, 1907. Vol. 7, no. 24.

———. "Eagles Organize and Have Big Spread." March 12, 1909.

———. "Fire Destroys Big Craig Hotel." November 15, 1915.

———. "Gambling Prohibited." May 4, 1906. www.coloradohistoricnewspapers.org. Accessed October 6, 2009.

———. "Getting Ready to Incorporate." March 15, 1907. www.coloradohistoricnewspapers.org. Accessed October 25, 2009.

———. "Good Citizenship, Republican Slogan." April 2, 1915. www.coloradohistoricnewspapers.org. Accessed September 24, 2009.

———. "Grand Jury Starts General Clean Up of Bootlegging and Gambling." January 12, 1917.

———. "In Jail after Baggs Auto Trip." July 13, 1917.

———. January 31, 1908. www.coloradohistoricnewspapers.org. Accessed February 13, 2009.

———. "Jim Ray Killed by His Wife." November 12, 1915. www.coloradohistoricnewspapers.org. Accessed October 1, 2013.

———. "Jungle News from Brooklyn." October 15, 1909. www.coloradohistoricnewspapers.org. Accessed June 19, 2013.

———. "Knocks and Boosts." March 31, 1911.

———. "Local and Personal Doings." September 8, 1905. www.coloradohistoricnewspapers.org. Accessed September 30, 2009.

————. "Local News of the Week." August 27, 1915. www.coloradohistoricnewspapers.org. Accessed September 30, 2009.

————. "Meeting of the Dads." November 16, 1900. www.coloradohistoricnewspapers.org. Accessed October 4, 2009.

————. "Merritt-McQuarrie." April 25, 1919. www.coloradohistoricnewspapers.org. Accessed February 17, 2009.

————. "Much Property Lost in Two Bad Fires." November 27, 1914.

————. "Old Landmark Disappears." October 22, 1920.

————. "An Ordinance." August 21, 1903. www.coloradohistoricnewspapers.org. Accessed October 4, 2009.

————. "Pin Ears Mastered in Denver Exhibition." June 16, 1905.

————. "A Poor Shot." March 22, 1912.

————. "Pure Local Notes." March 1, 1907. www.coloradohistoricnewspapers.org. Accessed October 4, 2009.

————. "Ray Murder Case." November 19, 1915. www.coloradohistoricnewspapers.org. Accessed July 24, 2013.

————. "Realty Transfers." May 17, 1912. www.coloradohistoricnewspapers.org. Accessed February 17, 2009.

————. "Rev. Mr. Evans Was in Court." January 1, 1909. www.coloradohistoricnewspapers.org. Accessed September 21, 2009.

————. "Shooting Affray." June 12, 1908.

————. "Slashed Almost Into Ribbons." February 3, 1911.

————. "Splendid New Ticket." March 26, 1909.

————. "Temperance Work." September 8, 1911. www.coloradohistoricnewspapers.org. Accessed October 4, 2009.

————. "Town Board." April 29, 1904. www.coloradohistoricnewspapers.org. Accessed October 7, 2009.

————. "The Town Board." August 15, 1902. www.coloradohistoricnewspapers.org. Accessed October 6, 2009.

————. "Town Board." September 4, 1903. www.coloradohistoricnewspapers.org. Accessed October 4, 2009.

————. "Town Board Meeting." June 21, 1901. www.coloradohistoricnewspapers.org. Accessed October 6, 2009.

————. "When the Moffat Road Comes In." January 1, 1904. www.coloradohistoricnewspapers.org. Accessed October 9, 2013.

*Routt National Forest History.* CO: U.S. Forest Service Reports, 1948.

Rutter, M. *Upstairs Girls: Prostitution in the American West.* Helena, MT: Far Country Press, 2005.

*Silver Cliff Rustler.* "Moffat Road Financed." June 25, 1902. www.coloradohistoricnewspapers.org. Accessed June 5, 2013.

Spooner, G.A. "Mt. Harris." *Steamboat Pilot*, March 16, 1927.

Stanko, Jim, Sureva Towler and Judy Seligson. *The Historical Guide to Routt County.* CO: Tread of Pioneers Museum, 1979.

*Steamboat Pilot.* "Boxing Contest." June 26, 1907.

————. "Burt Discharged; Reidy and Companions on Trial." March 4, 1914. www.coloradohistoricnewspapers.org. Accessed June 4, 2013.

————. "Committees Named for Pioneer Day Celebration." August 2, 1911.

————. "County Commissioners." October 14, 1896.

————. "County News." August 12, 1908.

————. "The County Records." March 1, 1905.

————. "Craig and Its Splendid Resources." March 30, 1910.

————. "District Court Will Open Here Monday April 3." March 23, 1939.

————. "History and Members of the Pioneer Association." September 1, 1909.

————. "It Is Up to Steamboat." January 10, 1906. www.coloradohistoricnewspapers. org. Accessed November 8, 2009.

————. "James Ray Killed When His Wife Uses Revolver." November 10, 1915. www.coloradohistoricnewspapers.org. Accessed August 31, 2013.

————. "Laying the Rails." June 24, 1903. www.coloradohistoricnewspapers.org. Accessed August 12, 2013.

————. "Many Charges Grow Out of Oak Creek Shooting." February 25, 1914. www.coloradohistoricnewspapers.org. Accessed June 24, 2013.

————. "May Ray Guilty." June 13, 1917. www.coloradohistoricnewspapers.org. Accessed October 10, 2013.

————. "May Ray Won Her Freedom by Nursing Influenza Victims." October 1, 1919.

————. "McAlpine-Williams Mill Was a Hot One." December 20, 1905.

————. "Mrs. Louisa Piercen." January 4, 1929.

————. "Murder in the Second Degree Is Jury Findings." January 19, 1916.

————. "The New Liquor Ordinance." June 1901.

————. "The New Moffat Road." June 1902. www.coloradohistoricnewspapers. org. Accessed October 3, 2013.

————. "Officers Who Guided Routt County in the Early Days of Its History." September 2, 1925.

————. "Opening of the New Era." February 28, 1906. www.coloradohistoricnewspapers. org. Accessed October 30, 2009.

————. "Ordinance." November 21, 1900. www.coloradohistoricnewspapers.org. Accessed February 1, 2009.

————. "Realty Transfers." May 10, 1910. www.coloradohistoricnewspapers.org. Accessed October 16, 2009.

————. "Recalls a Tragedy." March 8, 1916. www.coloradohistoricnewspapers.org. Accessed May 20, 2013.

————. "Routt County Carnival." September 2, 1903. www.coloradohistoricnewspapers. org. Accessed October 25, 2009.

————. "Shorty Anderson Dead at Pershing." February 24, 1928.

————. "Steamboat Celebration Will Be Biggest Ever." June 25, 1913.

————. "Steamboat Springs!" January 2, 1889. www.coloradohistoricnewspapers. org. Accessed October 19, 2009.

————. "Steamboat Springs Past, Present and Future." February 28, 1906.

————. "Tales of Early Days." April 28, 1915.

————. "Tales of the Early Days." June 11, 1913.

————. "Tales of the Old West." November 5, 1936.

————. "Talking 'Game Day.'" July 12, 1899. www.coloradohistoricnewspapers. org. Accessed October 25, 2009.

————. "'Tex' Williams Is Dead from Accidental Wound." September 29, 1901.

————. "Thomas Piercen, Colorado Pioneer Dies at Age of 74." March 1, 1945. www.coloradohistoricnewspapers.org. Accessed September 14, 2013.

————. "Town Goes Wet." July 5, 1916. www.coloradohistoricnewspapers.org. Accessed August 31, 2013.

————. "Visited Brooklyn: Well Known Politician Rides the 'Booze Wagon,'" July 18, 1906.

————. "Watch Oak Creek Grow," April 28, 1915.

Stukey, Leona. "Scholars Write of Steamboat." *Steamboat Pilot*, February 28, 1906.

United States Penitentiary for Colorado. Joseph Ward, Colorado Archives.

U.S. Census 1910 Colorado 21ˢᵗ Precinct. ancestry.com. Accessed February 9, 2009.

*Wind River Mountaineer*. "Former Wyoming Man Killed at Ely, Nevada." February 11, 1916.

Wren, J. "The Shady Side of the River." *Steamboat Magazine* 6, no. 2 (1984): 30–31.

*Yampa Leader*. "Huggins Is Enjoined." May 4, 1907. www.coloradohistoricnewspapers. org. Accessed October 20, 2013.

————. "Huggins Now a City." February 16, 1907.

————. "James Ray Fatally Shot by His Wife." November 12, 1915. www. coloradohistoricnewspapers.org. Accessed March 8, 2013.

————. "Legal Notices." June 2, 1906.

————. "License Hiked to $1,000." January 17, 1913.

————. "Local News." February 5, 1909.

————. "Local News." January 1, 1909.

————. "Local News." May 14, 1909.

————. "The Royal Changes Hands." July 21, 1906.

————. "Special Town Meeting." February 22, 1908.

Yurich, Mike. *Oak Creek Colorado: The Corner of Main and Sharpe*. Oak Creek, CO: Tracks and Trails Museum, 1967.

# INDEX

# INDEX

# ABOUT THE AUTHOR

Laurel Watson lives in Steamboat Springs with her family and is the curator at the Hayden Heritage Center Museum in the nearby town of Hayden. Her passions include genealogy, local history and historical preservation, and she serves as a board member of Historic Routt County and as historical consultant of West Routt County for Northwest Colorado Heritage Tourism. She has written a number of articles on local history that have appeared in the *Yampa Valley Voice*, *Steamboat Magazine* and *Steamboat Today* and has given public talks on various local history subjects, including the Brooklyn red-light district. She has a BA in social science and history, as well as an MA degree in American history from Regis University, Denver, and has adjunct taught at Colorado Northwestern Community College and Colorado Mountain College.